NAVIGATING LEAN DIGITAL TRANSFORMATION

Trusted Globally by Lean and Digital Leaders

NAVIGATING LEAN DIGITAL TRANSFORMATION

People First, Tech Second

GOURAV DUDEJA

ISBN
Paperback 979-8-89475-256-3
Hardcase 979-8-89475-300-3

Contents

Part One

Before we start: Let's Understand

Lean Digital - A Do or Die?

Part Two

Focus One: Customer & Strategy

Customer vs. CEOs vs. Leaders - Is it a Priority Gap?

Part Three

Focus Two: Benchmarking - What's happening in the world?

Lean Digital - A Key Enabler, A Buzz or A Lipstick?

Part Four

Focus Three: It's a people Game

Why is it everyone's responsibility?

Part Five

Focus Four: Technology is Process Enabler only

Why 90% Digital Transformation fails?

Introduction
Truth That Everyone Can Relate

It's no secret that the unprecedented hurdles that businesses face in today's extremely fast digital world are having a serious effect on their bottom lines. In today's fast-paced, constantly changing global economy, the old ways of doing business just don't cut it. Because of this, many businesses are adopting a strategy known as "Lean Digital Transformation" to propel transformation and generate long-term success.

Lean Digital transformation is an approach that seeks to enhance productivity by streamlining processes, reducing waste, and encouraging a mindset of constant refinement. Lean principles can be applied to digital transformation to help businesses save money, increase efficiency, and create better goods and services.

Organisational silos are a major problem in the modern digital world. When departments in an organisation don't communicate with one another, inefficiency, duplication of effort, and mistakes pile up. Information is not shared across the organisation, which results in inefficient decision-making and slow implementation due to silos.

One huge financial institution, for instance, was losing a lot of money because of all the silos it had set up. There was a lot of wasted time and energy since different divisions weren't sharing information with one another. As a result of the CEO's foresight, a Lean Digital transformation initiative has been started. The company was able to significantly increase its bottom line once it eliminated silos and streamlined its operations.

Slow execution is another problem that many businesses confront. In today's digital age, where speed is of the essence, businesses that are sluggish to respond risk falling behind the competition. Legacy systems, which are sometimes slow and complicated, are a major obstacle for many businesses.

As an illustration, a major retail chain was falling behind the competition because of its reliance on antiquated legacy technologies. As a result of the CEO's foresight, a Lean Digital transformation initiative has been launched. The company gained an edge in the market by increasing its speed of execution thanks to technology and process upgrades.

Lack of trust in new hires and legacy staff is also a major contributor to the high turnover rates that many businesses are experiencing. Lack of trust can lead to miscommunication, lower production, and lower earnings.

There was a lot of turnover at one major computer firm because people just didn't trust each other. As a result of the CEO's foresight, a Lean Digital transformation initiative has been launched. The company's attrition rates dropped and its profits rose because of its emphasis on trust and teamwork. Conflicts with other executives are also a source of stress for CEOs and can negatively affect teamwork and decision-making. Organisations can reduce tensions and encourage teamwork by adopting lean practises for digital transformation.

Finally, many businesses invest heavily in staff training but fail to match that investment with enough office space. The pressure to hit key performance indicators and set goals might cause people to prioritise short-term gains over long-term achievements.

In sum, Lean Digital transformation is an effective method for adapting to the difficulties of the digital era. Organisations can enhance their bottom line and enjoy sustained growth if they prioritise streamlining processes, getting rid of unnecessary steps, and encouraging a mindset of constant improvement.

Agree Or Not, But That's Why Lean Digital Fails

1. Organisational setup that prevents effective communication and collaboration between lean and digital teams, known as "functional silos."

2. Priorities aren't aligned, which causes problems with resource allocation and inadequate results from lean and digital projects.

3. A lack of a comprehensive plan for Lean Digital transformation has led to scattered efforts and an absence of leadership.

4. Organisational reluctance to adopt digital technology and lean practises is a major barrier to their effective implementation, as is employee resistance to such changes.

5. The lack of strong leadership and commitment to achieving Lean Digital transformation, which in turn leads to a lack of incentive and responsibility, brings us to point number five.

6. Lack of programmes to train and develop workers to ensure they have the appropriate lean and digital competences is problem number six.

7. Siloed decision-making procedures and restricted cross-functional cooperation, hindering the integration of lean and digital efforts, are the seventh barrier to lean and digital adoption.

8. There aren't enough key performance indicators (KPIs) in place to track how well Lean Digital projects are doing or how much of an impact they're having.

9. Not doing enough to overcome resistance and provide a seamless transition to Lean Digital practises.

10. Overlooking the long-term benefits and scalability of a Lean Digital deployment in favour of rapid outcomes and gains.

Purpose Of This Book

"You have been told a lie -
Lean and Digital can work without each other."

In this ever changing era, organizations are failing to meet the needs of digital transformation and so are undergoing various changes to grow themselves. One among these changes includes inculcating more lean and digital leaders, thus promoting lean and digital at their organization.

But do you think lean and digital leaders are doing the same job? Are they sitting on the same chair of responsibilities? The answer is no!

Lean leaders think differently, work differently and talk differently compared to digital leaders.

They prefer to stay connected with people, are not much into technology and remain grounded.

Whereas digital leaders are not much connected with people, are all the time into technology and think lean is not their cup of tea.

And that's the most considerable confusion between lean and digital. For an organization to transform successfully, lean and digital should sync.

If this is so, then why not combine lean and digital? Yes, we have done it for you by introducing which aims to help leaders in organizations to make their lean and digital journey successful.

So, stop scratching your head and turn the pages to become the master of lean and digital.

This book is for	This book is not for
👤 Lean leaders	👤 People who are focused only on the result rather than culture
👤 Digital leaders	👤 Those that do not desire to achieve success in their life
👤 Business executives	👤 People who do not want to grow their organization
👤 All levels employees including CXO's, EVP's & more	

Part One

Before we start: Let's Understand

Lean Digital – A Do or Die?

"Quality is the result of a carefully constructed cultural environment. It has to be the fabric of the organization, not part of the fabric."

~Philip Crosby

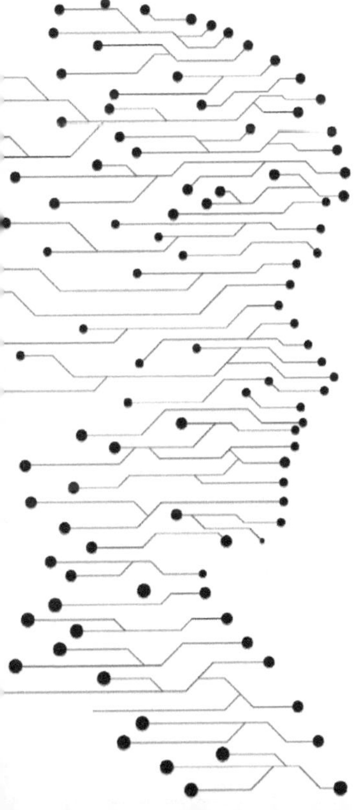

In recent years, the business landscape has changed dramatically with the rise of digital technologies and the fast-paced evolution of the market. Companies are under constant pressure to keep up with these changes and remain competitive. The good news is that there is a proven approach to help businesses navigate this transformation - Lean Digital.

When problems arise during digital transformation, it is usual for employees to offer explanations to managerial staff. Unanticipated technological difficulties, higher-than-expected costs, high attrition rates, and opposition to change are only some of the possible justifications. However, in many circumstances, these justifications are really a means for staff to cover up the underlying causes of delays or failures on the project.

According to a McKinsey & Company report, the most prevalent reasons of digital transformation failures are a lack of employee engagement and ineffective change management practises. Employees were not completely committed to the digital transformation strategy, and they were not given the time or resources to make the move.

Furthermore, according to Harvard Business Review study, misalignment between business and IT goals is a primary factor to the failure of digital transformation initiatives. This mismatch causes delays, cost overruns, and other issues, which are then blamed on factors such as moving technology or unanticipated impediments. To stop this kind of behaviour, businesses should make sure they know their employees well enough to address their worries and give them the resources they need to make the shift to digital transformation as painless as possible. Spending money on change management initiatives, educating and training staff, and encouraging openness and responsibility are all examples of this. In conclusion, when a digital transformation project runs into trouble, it's just natural for employees to offer up explanations. However, it's vital for businesses to look past these explanations and get to the bottom of the problems. They can tackle these problems head-on and complete the Lean Digital Transformation if they do so.

1.1.1 Let's Align Our Basics Here:

- **What is Lean, what is Digital, and what if you combine them together?**

Lean is a management philosophy that emphasizes eliminating waste in all processes and operations. The focus is on delivering value to the customer with the least number of resources possible. Many organizations in various industries, including manufacturing, healthcare, and service sectors, have adopted this approach.

Digital, on the other hand, refers to the use of technology to automate and streamline processes, increase Efficiency, and improve communication and collaboration. The rise of digital technologies has dramatically changed the way businesses operate, and organizations are now expected to adopt digital solutions to remain competitive.

Lean Digital is a combination of the Lean philosophy and digital technology. The Lean philosophy originated in the manufacturing industry and is centred around eliminating waste in all processes and operations, focusing on delivering value to the customer using the least amount of resources possible. Digital technology, on the other hand, automates and streamlines processes, increases Efficiency, and improves communication and collaboration. By combining these two approaches, companies can optimize their digital operations and maximize their impact.

The Lean philosophy has been adopted by a variety of industries, including manufacturing, healthcare, and service sectors, and has proven to be effective in maximizing efficiency and reducing waste. The Lean Digital approach provides a roadmap for companies to successfully navigate this digital transformation, combining the principles of Lean with the power of technology.

- **Why is Lean Digital critical for business success?**

The digital revolution has brought about new challenges and opportunities for companies. Companies must adopt digital solutions and adapt to new technologies to remain competitive. However, the shift to digital can be daunting for many organizations, as it requires a significant time investment, resources, and money. This is where Lean Digital comes in - it provides a framework for companies to make the most of their digital transformation efforts.

By adopting the Lean philosophy, companies can eliminate waste and maximize efficiency in their digital operations. This frees up resources that can be used to invest in new technologies, improve customer experiences, and stay ahead of the competition. The focus on delivering value to the customer is also a critical component of the Lean Digital approach, as it ensures that companies meet their target audience's needs and expectations.

In addition, Lean Digital also helps companies prioritize their digital initiatives, ensuring that they are focused on the most important projects and initiatives that will significantly impact their business. This helps companies avoid the trap of trying too much at once and enables them to focus on the initiatives that will impact their business the most. In this chapter, we will delve into the essence of Lean Digital, explore why it is a do-or-die for businesses today, and provide practical lessons on how companies can implement it in their own organizations.

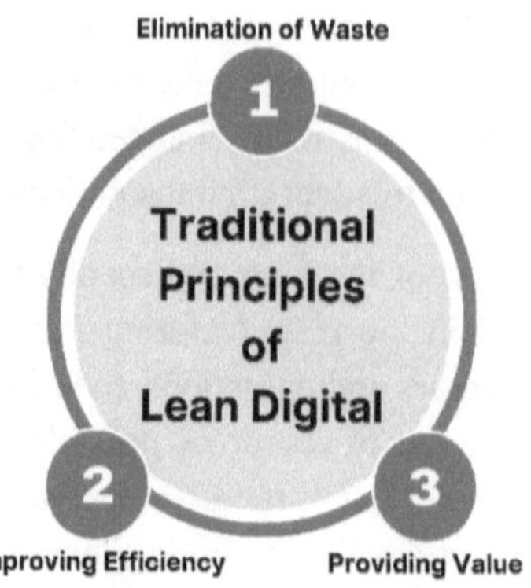

Figure 1: Traditional Principles of Lean Digital

- **Traditional Principles of Lean Digital**

Lean Digital is a systematic and effective approach to optimizing digital operations, which emphasizes on three key principles, which are:

1. Elimination of Waste

Lean Digital prioritizes the elimination of all forms of waste in digital operations. This includes the elimination of waste in time, money, and resources. By reducing waste, organizations can reduce costs, increase the impact of their digital operations, and improve their bottom line. This is a critical aspect of Lean Digital as it helps organizations to focus on what is truly important and to eliminate any inefficiencies or unnecessary steps in their processes.

Waste can take many forms, including duplicated efforts, unnecessary steps in processes, and the use of outdated technology or tools. Lean Digital encourages organizations to identify and eliminate waste through continuous improvement and the adoption of best practices in digital operations. This can be achieved through a number of techniques, such as process mapping, value stream mapping, and Lean Six Sigma.

2. Providing Value

Lean Digital is focused on providing maximum value to customers through digital operations. This can be in the form of quality, speed, or cost. By prioritizing customer value, organizations can ensure that their digital operations are aligned with their business objectives and meet the needs of their customers.

One of the key aspects of Lean Digital is understanding customers' needs and gathering feedback to improve the organization's digital operations continuously. This feedback can be gathered through surveys, customer service interactions, and other methods. By incorporating this feedback into the organization's digital operations, organizations can ensure that they are meeting the needs of their customers and providing maximum value.

3. Improving Efficiency

Lean Digital aims to improve Efficiency in digital operations. This includes improving processes, reducing errors, and increasing productivity. Organizations can reduce costs, increase competitiveness, and provide a better customer experience by improving Efficiency.

Improving efficiency can be achieved through a number of techniques, such as process mapping, Lean Six Sigma, and the adoption of new technologies. Lean Digital encourages organizations to evaluate their processes and identify areas for improvement continually. By continuously improving their processes, organizations can reduce waste, increase Efficiency, and provide a better customer experience.

Business Case Example

David is an employee at ABC Corporation, a mid-sized organization that distributes consumer goods.

David recognized the need for digital transformation in the organization to remain competitive in the market. However, other employees and digital leaders were coming up with excuses that digital transformation requires a lot of training, it is expensive, time-consuming, and not feasible for a mid-sized organization like ABC Corporation.

The organization has struggled to improve its processes and efficiency due to resistance to digital transformation. Employees and digital leaders were skeptical about the feasibility and benefits of digital transformation in a mid-sized organization.

Despite these obstacles, David decided to take the lead and successfully implemented digital transformation in the organization. He thoroughly analyzed the organization's processes, developed a digital transformation strategy, and communicated the benefits of digital transformation to all employees and stakeholders, including customers and suppliers.

To implement the proposed solution, David established a digital transformation team consisting of employees from various departments.

Implementing digital solutions improved the organization's processes, reduced costs, and enhanced customer experience. The organization also identified new business opportunities through digital solutions. Employees' involvement in the digital transformation process created a sense of ownership and commitment, resulting in a more engaged workforce.

David's efforts resulted in the successful digital transformation of ABC Corporation.

Take Away- *Misconceptions surrounding Lean and Digitalization can hinder an organization's ability to improve its processes and efficiency.*

- **Identifying and eliminating digital waste**

Unnecessary complexity: Overly complex digital processes and systems can lead to waste in terms of time and resources. By simplifying these processes, companies can reduce waste and improve Efficiency.

Duplication of effort: When multiple departments or teams are working on the same tasks, it can lead to duplication of effort and waste. By improving collaboration between teams, companies can reduce waste and increase Efficiency.

Inefficient processes: Poorly designed processes and systems can lead to inefficiency and waste. By improving these processes, companies can reduce waste and improve the overall impact of their digital operations.

Once digital waste has been identified, companies can take steps to eliminate it. This can involve streamlining processes, reducing complexity, and improving team collaboration. By reducing digital waste, companies can increase efficiency, reduce costs, and improve the overall impact of their digital operations.

- **Implementing Lean Digital in the Workplace**

To successfully implement Lean Digital principles in the workplace, companies need to prioritize a commitment to change across all levels of the organization and the integration of Lean Digital principles into day-to-day operations. Some steps companies can take to implement Lean Digital include:

1. **Adopting best practices:** Companies can adopt best practices in digital operations, such as continuous improvement, in order to optimize their digital operations. Companies can stay ahead of the curve by continuously improving their digital operations and remaining competitive.

2. **Improving processes:** Companies can streamline and automate processes, reduce complexity, and increase collaboration between teams. This will help reduce waste and increase efficiency in digital operations.

3. **Empowering teams:** Teams must be empowered to take ownership of their digital operations and to implement Lean Digital principles. This can involve providing them with the necessary training and tools and creating a culture that supports continuous improvement.

4. **Encouraging feedback:** Companies must encourage feedback from customers and employees to identify areas for improvement in digital operations. This feedback can be used to make necessary changes and improve the overall impact of digital operations.

5. **Measuring success:** Companies must establish metrics to measure the success of their Lean Digital implementation. These metrics can include the following:

6. **Customer satisfaction:** Measuring the level of customer satisfaction with the digital operations and services offered.

7. **Time savings:** Measuring the time savings achieved through the streamlining of processes and the elimination of waste.

8. **Cost savings:** Measuring the cost savings achieved through the elimination of waste and improvement in efficiency.

Companies can track their progress and adjust their approach as needed by regularly monitoring these metrics. This continuous improvement approach is a key principle of Lean Digital and helps ensure the long-term success of the implementation.

Key Takeaways

Lean Digital is a well-structured approach to digital transformation that prioritizes eliminating waste, providing value, and improving efficiency in digital operations.

By combining the principles of Lean with the power of technology, organizations can optimize their digital operations and maximize their impact.

Lean Digital provides a roadmap for companies to navigate digital transformation successfully, and its three key principles - elimination of waste, providing value, and improving efficiency - are critical components for business success in the digital era.

Adopting the Lean Digital approach can help organizations prioritize their digital initiatives, eliminate inefficiencies, and ensure that they are meeting the needs and expectations of their customers.

1.2 Lean Digital Fails - Politics or Capability Gaps?

Lean Digital involves streamlining processes, eliminating waste, and improving quality through a continuous improvement cycle. However, despite its popularity, many organizations still struggle to achieve the desired results with Lean Digital.

The two most common causes of failure in Lean Digital transformation are capability gaps and excessive politics between departments. These issues may hinder the implementation of Lean Digital projects, making it impossible for the company to realise its transformation objectives. One common situation is intense rivalry between various parts of an organisation. This can lead to individuals or groups putting their personal goals ahead of those of the Lean Digital project as a whole. Delays, misunderstandings, and a lack of alignment could originate from their power conflict, withholding of information, and resistance to working together. This kind of conduct can undermine Lean Digital Transformation's fundamental tenets—cross-departmental cooperation and a unified goal.

Internal shortages of skills present yet another obstacle. Some people may be resistant to acquiring or developing new abilities, despite the fact that they are necessary in the modern digital world. They could be reluctant to learn and adapt, scared of new technologies, or resistant to change. This inability may hinder the company's efforts to adopt Lean Digital practises and keep it from realising digital technology's full potential.

In a large manufacturing company, politics have been shown to block Lean Digital transformation. The organisation's various departments had competing goals and aims. They fought amongst themselves for control rather than working together towards a common digital goal, and they avoided working together on cross-departmental projects. The company's digital transformation initiatives stopped, and the advantages of adopting Lean Digital principles were not fully exploited.

Another instance included a financial institution that struggled to perform a Lean Digital transformation due to skill shortages. In spite of the company's investment in cutting-edge IT infrastructure and software, many workers lacked the expertise to make effective use of these resources. The organisation's digital objectives and its actual capabilities are vastly different because certain employees refused training and upskilling opportunities.

Organisational cultures that encourage teamwork, openness, and lifelong education are essential for meeting these problems. They should foster interdisciplinary teamwork, offer professional development opportunities, and cultivate an atmosphere where employees are motivated to accept and adapt to change and learn new digital skills.

1.2.1 Political factors in Lean Digital

In today's fast-paced digital world, Lean Digital has emerged as a popular approach to optimize business processes and improve customer satisfaction. However, political factors and capability gaps can significantly impact the success of Lean Digital projects. Let's explore the political factors and capability gaps that can hinder Lean Digital initiatives and discuss effective strategies to overcome them.

- **Resistance to change**

One of the main political factors that can impact the success of Lean Digital projects is resistance to change. This can come from various stakeholders, including employees, customers, suppliers, regulators, and competitors. Resistance to change can arise from fear of losing power, status, or job security, from lack of trust in the new technology or process, from unfamiliarity with the new way of working, or from conflicting interests or values. To overcome resistance to change, Lean Digital practitioners need to engage in effective communication, stakeholder alignment, and change management. They need to explain the benefits and risks of the new digital solution, solicit feedback and suggestions, and address any concerns or objections. They also need to empower and enable employees and customers to embrace and adopt the new solution and to create a culture of innovation and continuous improvement.

- **Political maneuvering**

Another political factor that can impact the success of Lean Digital projects is political maneuvering. This can involve actors who seek to advance their own interests and gain influence or control over the project. Political maneuvering can occur at various levels, from the project team to the business unit, the company, the industry, or the sector. Political maneuvering can result in misaligned objectives, conflicting priorities, or sabotaged decisions or actions. To counteract political maneuvering, Lean Digital practitioners need to foster transparency, accountability, and trust. They need to establish clear roles, responsibilities, and expectations for all stakeholders and align the project objectives with the company strategy and goals. They also need to involve stakeholders in the project decision-making, design, and delivery processes and seek feedback and input at regular intervals.

- **Power struggles**

A third political factor that can impact the success of Lean Digital projects is power struggles. This can involve actors who compete for control, influence, or recognition over the project. Power struggles can occur between the project team and the business unit, between different business units, between the company and its partners, or between the company and its competitors. Power struggles can result in delayed decisions, conflicting mandates, or undermined resources or support. To resolve power struggles, Lean Digital practitioners need to create a shared vision and mission for the project and establish a governance model that ensures fair representation and participation of all stakeholders. They need to facilitate collaboration and cooperation and establish clear communication and decision-making lines. They also need to balance the interests and needs of the different stakeholders and leverage each stakeholder's strengths and capabilities to enhance the project outcomes.

1.2.2 Capability gaps in Lean Digital

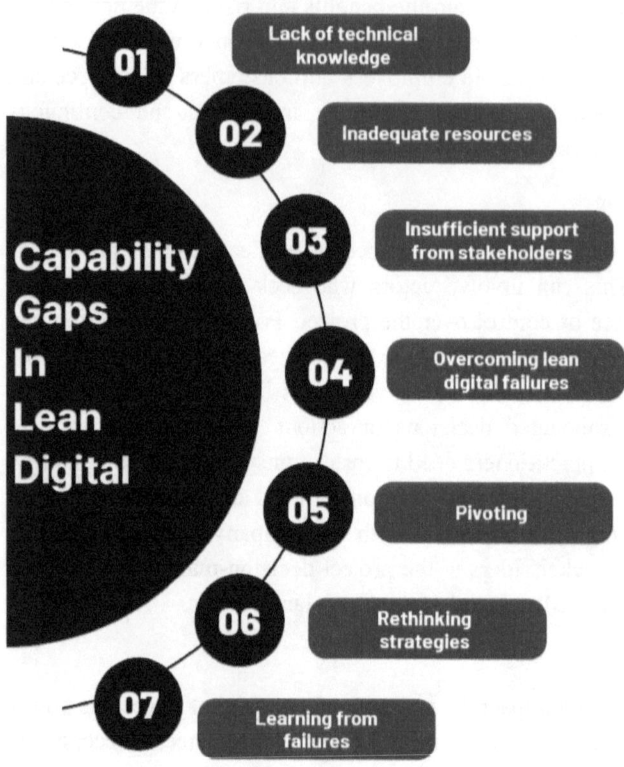

Figure 2: Capability gaps in Lean Digital

Capability gaps can hinder the success of Lean Digital projects and slow down progress. In this section, we will explore the different capability gaps that Lean Digital practitioners may face and learn how to address these gaps in order to ensure the success of their projects.

- **Lack of Technical Knowledge**

A lack of technical knowledge is one of the main capability gaps that can hinder the success of Lean Digital projects. This can involve the project team, business unit, company, industry, or sector. A lack of technical knowledge can result in poor quality, ineffective design, or incorrect implementation of the digital solution. To overcome the lack of technical knowledge, Lean Digital practitioners need to invest in training and development and seek expertise and guidance from internal or external sources. They need to adopt best practices and standards for digital innovation and leverage existing or new technologies and platforms that support Lean Digital. They also need to engage in continuous learning and improvement and seek feedback and input from customers, employees, and partners.

- **Inadequate Resources**

Another capability gap that can hinder the success of Lean Digital projects is inadequate resources. This can include a shortage of budget, manpower, or equipment. Inadequate resources can result in slow progress, low quality, or insufficient support for the digital solution. To address inadequate resources, Lean Digital practitioners need to prioritize their projects and allocate resources based on their importance, urgency, and potential impact. They need to optimize their processes and practices to reduce waste and inefficiencies. They also need to seek alternative sources of funding, talent, or technology to leverage partnerships and collaborations to enhance their results.

- **Insufficient Support from Stakeholders**

A third capability gap that can hinder the success of Lean Digital projects is insufficient support from stakeholders. This can include a lack of commitment, interest, or involvement from the project team, the business unit, the company, or the industry or sector. Insufficient support from stakeholders can result in low morale, poor performance, or lack of buy-in for the digital solution. To enhance support from stakeholders, Lean Digital practitioners need to engage in active communication and stakeholder management. They need to understand the interests and needs of each stakeholder to align the project objectives with their expectations and requirements. They also need to involve stakeholders in the project design and delivery processes to seek their feedback and input at regular intervals.

- **Overcoming Lean Digital Failures**

Failure is a part of the innovation process, but Lean Digital practitioners can overcome failures by applying specific strategies. In this section, we will discuss the strategies for overcoming Lean Digital failures, including pivoting, rethinking strategies, and learning from failures. By using these strategies, Lean Digital practitioners can increase the chances of success for their initiatives.

- **Pivoting**

Pivoting is a critical strategy for overcoming Lean Digital failures. It involves changing the direction or focus of a project based on new information, insights, or feedback. This flexibility enables Lean Digital practitioners to adapt to changing circumstances and seize new opportunities while avoiding potential obstacles. By pivoting, Lean Digital practitioners can enhance the value and impact of their digital solutions, as well as optimize their results.

- **Rethinking Strategies**

Rethinking strategies is another important approach for overcoming Lean Digital failures. This involves revisiting the assumptions, hypotheses, and objectives of the project and reassessing the feasibility, viability, and desirability of the digital solution. By doing so, Lean Digital practitioners can identify and address the root causes of their failures and improve the chances of success for their initiatives. Additionally, rethinking strategies allows Lean Digital practitioners to better align their projects with the needs and expectations of their customers, employees, and partners.

- **Learning from Failures**

Finally, learning from failures is a key strategy for overcoming Lean Digital failures. This involves reflecting on the lessons learned from the project, including both the successes and failures, and applying these lessons to future projects. By learning from failures, Lean Digital practitioners can avoid repeating the same mistakes and improve their skills and knowledge. Additionally, learning from failures helps to enhance their resilience, creativity, and innovation, which are all essential qualities for successful Lean Digital practitioners.

Addressing capability gaps and overcoming failures are crucial steps in achieving success in Lean Digital projects. As technology continues to advance and the digital landscape evolves, Lean Digital practitioners must remain agile and adaptable in their approach. By investing in training and development, prioritizing resources, and engaging stakeholders, they can mitigate capability gaps and increase support for their initiatives. Furthermore, by applying the strategies of pivoting, rethinking strategies, and learning from failures, they can overcome setbacks and optimize their results.

1.2.3 Industry Case Studies in Lean Digital

In order to better understand the impact of political and capability factors on Lean Digital projects, it is useful to examine case studies from different industries. By exploring real-world examples, we can learn from the successes and failures of others and apply these insights to our initiatives.

- **Healthcare Industry**

In the healthcare industry, Lean Digital projects can have a significant impact on patient outcomes and the overall efficiency of healthcare delivery. For example, the use of telemedicine and electronic health records (EHRs) can improve the accessibility and quality of medical services while reducing the costs and risks associated with traditional healthcare delivery. However, the healthcare industry is also subject to complex political and regulatory environments, which can impact the success of Lean Digital projects. For instance, resistance to change can arise from concerns over the privacy and security of patient data, while political maneuvering can occur between different stakeholders in the healthcare delivery system, such as insurance companies, hospitals, and pharmaceutical companies.

- **Retail Industry**

In the retail industry, Lean Digital projects can transform the shopping experience for consumers and improve the competitiveness of retailers. For instance, the use of mobile and online shopping, omnichannel fulfilment, and personalized marketing can create new opportunities for retailers to engage with customers and grow their businesses. However, the retail industry is also subject to rapidly changing consumer preferences and technological advancements, which can impact the success of Lean Digital projects. For example, the lack of technical knowledge can arise from the need to keep up with the latest digital trends and innovations, while inadequate resources can occur from the high costs associated with digital transformation initiatives.

- **Financial Services Industry**

Lean Digital projects can improve the efficiency, security, and customer experience of financial transactions and services in the financial services industry. For instance, the use of digital currencies, blockchain, and artificial intelligence (AI) can enhance the speed and accuracy of financial transactions while reducing the costs and risks associated with traditional financial services. However, the financial services industry is also subject to strict regulations and security standards, which can impact the success of Lean Digital projects. For example, resistance to change can arise from concerns over the privacy and security of financial data, while political maneuvering can occur between different stakeholders in the financial services sector, such as banks, insurance companies, and regulators.

- **Transportation Industry**

In the transportation industry, Lean Digital projects can transform how people move, and goods are transported, creating new opportunities for efficiency and sustainability. For instance, using autonomous vehicles, smart transportation systems, and electric vehicles can improve transportation safety and speed while reducing transportation costs and environmental impact. However, the transportation industry is also subject to rapidly evolving technological advancements and regulatory environments, which can impact the success of Lean Digital projects. For example, the lack of technical knowledge can arise from the need to keep up with the latest developments in autonomous vehicle technology, while inadequate resources can occur from the high costs associated with digital transformation initiatives.

These industry case studies demonstrate the challenges and opportunities that Lean Digital practitioners face in different sectors and the importance of understanding the political and capability factors that impact the success of their projects. By applying the strategies and lessons learned from these examples, Lean Digital practitioners can increase their chances of success and improve the outcomes of their initiatives.

Key Takeaways

Lean Digital is a powerful methodology that can help organizations drive digital innovation, reduce waste, and minimize risk. However, Lean Digital projects can still face challenges and fail due to political and capability gaps.

Political factors such as resistance to change, political maneuvering, and power struggles can impact the success of Lean Digital initiatives. Capability gaps, such as a lack of technical knowledge and inadequate resources, can also hinder the success of Lean Digital projects.

It is crucial for organizations to be aware of these challenges and take proactive measures to overcome them, such as fostering a supportive culture, empowering employees and customers, and investing in training and development. By doing so, organizations can increase the chances of success and reap the benefits of Lean Digital.

1.3 What is Lean Digital in The VUCA World?

Volatility, Uncertainty, Complexity, and Ambiguity (VUCA) describe the state of the world today. Market volatility, innovative technologies, and rising consumer demands all pose continual challenges to today's firms. Lean Digital transformation is a solution to this problem. It offers businesses a structure for improving efficiency, cutting down on waste, and increasing productivity with the use of digital tools.

In order to implement Lean Digital transformation in a VUCA environment, teamwork is essential. Progress can be slowed down by siloed functions and departmental thinking, which can also drive up costs. Conversely, teams that share a culture of cooperation are more likely to work together towards shared goals and build upon one another's knowledge to address difficult issues.

General Electric (GE) is an example of a company that has used Lean Digital transformation to thrive in a VUCA environment. The goal of GE's Digital Thread programme is to penetrate the entire organisation with digital technology, from product development to customer service. Data analytics, machine learning, and the IIoT are just a few examples of the digital technologies that GE has used to cut costs, boost quality, and boost production.

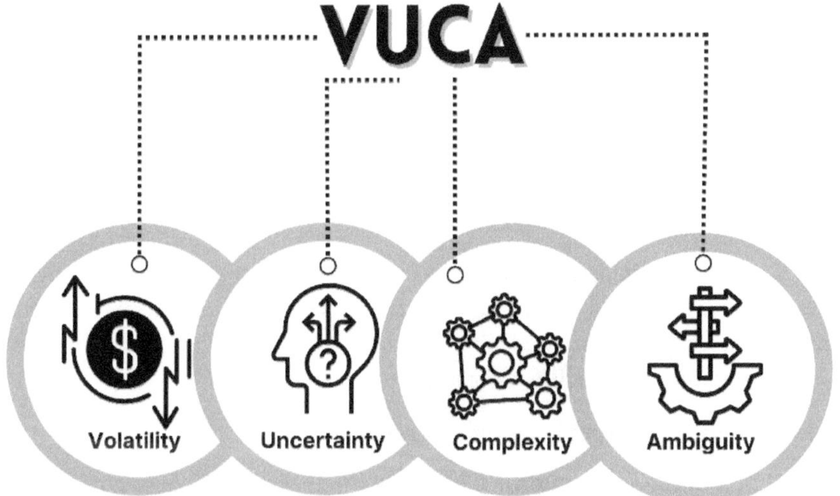

Figure 3: Lean Digital in VUCA World

1.3.1 Let's align our basics-

- **Understanding the VUCA world**

Have you ever felt overwhelmed by the rapidly changing business landscape? Have you struggled to keep up with the multitude of variables that impact your organization? If so, you are not alone. The business world has become increasingly unpredictable and complex, leading to the emergence of the VUCA world. But what exactly is the VUCA world, and how does it impact organizations like yours?

- **What is VUCA and what does the acronym stand for?**

The acronym VUCA was first coined in 1987 to describe four common challenges that one can face in the growing world. Since then it has been serving as a great point of orientation.

Volatility refers to the rapid and significant changes that occur in the business environment. These changes can come from a variety of sources, including changes in consumer behaviour, market trends, and technological advancements, among others. Organizations need to be able to quickly adapt to these changes and pivot their strategies as necessary to remain competitive.

Uncertainty refers to the lack of predictability and the difficulty in forecasting future outcomes. This can include economic conditions, government policies, and technological disruptions, among others. Organizations need to be able to make decisions and take action despite the Uncertainty, as not doing so can result in missed opportunities or significant losses.

Complexity refers to the intricate nature of the business environment and the relationships between various variables. This can include the number of stakeholders involved, the number of processes involved, and the number of variables that need to be taken into consideration. Organizations need to be able to navigate this complexity and make decisions quickly and effectively.

Ambiguity refers to the lack of clarity and difficulty in making decisions. This can include unclear regulations, ambiguous customer needs, and unclear market trends, among others. Organizations need to be able to make decisions despite the Ambiguity and effectively manage the risks associated with doing so.

- **Impact on the current business environment**

The VUCA world has a significant impact on the current business environment, making it increasingly challenging for organizations to maintain a competitive edge. Organizations need to be able to respond quickly to changes in the market and adapt their strategies accordingly. They also need to be able to take into consideration a greater number of variables, making decision-making more complex. The speed at which change is occurring and the number of variables that need to be taken into consideration makes it increasingly difficult for organizations to maintain a competitive edge.

- **Solving VUCA World problem with the Lean Digital approach**

The Lean Digital approach considers the VUCA factors and aims to improve the efficiency and effectiveness of processes while maintaining a focus on customer satisfaction. It leverages digital technology to eliminate waste and improve processes while also ensuring that the customer remains at the center of all decision-making. The Lean Digital approach is designed to help organizations navigate the VUCA world and remain competitive despite the challenges posed by this new reality.

1.3.2 Advantages of a Lean Digital approach in the VUCA World

The Lean Digital approach offers a number of advantages in the VUCA world. It allows organizations to respond quickly to changes in the market and adapt their strategies accordingly. This agility is crucial in the VUCA world, as organizations need to be able to pivot quickly to take advantage of new opportunities and overcome challenges. Additionally, by leveraging digital technology, the Lean Digital approach enables organizations to automate processes and eliminate waste, freeing up time and resources that can be used to focus on other areas of the business. This can result in improved efficiency and a more streamlined business process, leading to increased productivity and a more competitive edge. Major advantages are like:

1. Lean Digital approach focuses on customer satisfaction. By keeping the customer at the centre of all decision-making, organizations can ensure that they are providing the products and services that customers want and need. This not only leads to increased customer satisfaction but also helps to establish a strong and loyal customer base, which is crucial in the VUCA world, where customer loyalty can be difficult to maintain.

2. Lean Digital approach can also help organizations to manage the risks associated with the VUCA world. By automating processes and eliminating waste, organizations can reduce the risk of human error, which can have significant consequences in a rapidly changing business environment. Additionally, the Lean Digital approach can help organizations to make better decisions, as the use of data and technology can provide a clearer picture of the market and customer needs, allowing organizations to make informed decisions that take into consideration the VUCA factors.

3. It offers a solution to the challenges posed by the VUCA world. This approach takes into consideration the VUCA factors and aims to improve the efficiency and effectiveness of processes while still maintaining a focus on customer satisfaction. By leveraging digital technology, the Lean Digital approach enables organizations to automate processes and eliminate waste, freeing up time and resources that can be used to focus on other areas of the business. This can result in improved efficiency and a more streamlined business process, leading to increased productivity and a more competitive edge.

1.3.3 Challenges & Importance of Lean Digital in the VUCA World

The world of business is becoming increasingly unpredictable and volatile, making it difficult for organizations to maintain a competitive edge. This unpredictable and volatile environment has led to the development of the concept of the VUCA world, which refers to the volatile, uncertain, complex, and ambiguous (VUCA) environment that businesses currently find themselves in. The VUCA world poses significant challenges for organizations, as they need to be able to respond quickly to changes in the market and adapt their strategies accordingly. Additionally, they need to be able to navigate the complexity of the business environment and make decisions despite the ambiguity and uncertainty.

1. One of the key challenges faced by organizations in the VUCA world is volatility. Rapid and significant changes in the business environment can come from a variety of sources, including changes in consumer behaviour, market trends, and technological advancements, among others. Organizations need to be able to quickly adapt to these changes and pivot their strategies as necessary to remain competitive.

2. Another challenge posed by the VUCA world is uncertainty. The lack of predictability and the difficulty in forecasting future outcomes can make it difficult for organizations to make decisions and take action. This can include economic conditions, government policies, and technological disruptions, among others. Organizations need to be able to make decisions and take action despite the uncertainty, as not doing so can result in missed opportunities or significant losses.

3. Complexity is also a major challenge faced by organizations in the VUCA world. The intricate nature of the business environment and the relationships between various variables can make it difficult for organizations to navigate and make decisions quickly and effectively. This can include the number of stakeholders involved, the number of processes involved, and the number of variables that need to be taken into consideration.

4. Finally, ambiguity is a challenge that organizations face in the VUCA world. The lack of clarity and difficulty in making decisions can include unclear regulations, ambiguous customer needs, and unclear market trends, among others. Organizations need to be able to make decisions despite the ambiguity and effectively manage the risks associated with doing so.

Key Takeaways

The VUCA world is a rapidly changing and complex business environment that poses significant challenges to organizations.

The Lean Digital approach offers a solution to navigating this environment by improving efficiency, agility, and customer satisfaction while managing risks. By leveraging digital technology to automate processes and eliminate waste, organizations can streamline their operations and respond quickly to changes in the market.

Additionally, by keeping the customer at the center of all decision-making, organizations can ensure that they are providing products and services that meet their needs, leading to increased customer satisfaction and loyalty.

The Lean Digital approach is crucial in the VUCA world, as it allows organizations to remain competitive despite the challenges posed by this new reality.

1.4 Lean Digital Success- Rise of A New Era?

The digital age has brought about a sea change in the way businesses function. In order to stay ahead of the curve and remain relevant in this rapidly evolving landscape, companies must adopt a lean and digitized approach to their operations.

This chapter will provide a comprehensive overview of the four essential lessons of Lean Digital success and shed light on the dawn of a new era.

The shift to Lean Digital collaboration is more than just a fad; it represents a fundamental change in the way businesses operate. Its potential to propel modern businesses ahead in the digital age has been recognised by professionals in a wide range of fields. Lean Digital collaboration seems to be the buzzword of the moment, but is it here to stay?

The efficacy of Lean Digital collaboration has been acknowledged by prominent figures in the industry. The famous author of "The Lean Startup," Eric Ries, stresses the importance of combining lean concepts with digital technologies to foster a culture of continuous improvement and innovation. He thinks that businesses that adopt Lean Digital collaboration will be better able to deal with uncertainty and seize opportunities.

In addition, **McKinsey & Company**, a multinational management consulting organisation, examined the matter of digital transformation in depth and found that lean practises were crucial to the success of such endeavours. Lean Digital collaboration was associated with greater operational efficiency, enhanced customer experiences, and accelerated revenue growth for businesses.

Lean Digital collaboration's revolutionary potential is further illustrated through real-world experiences. Using industrial IoT and data analytics, **General Electric (GE)** set out on a "Lean Digital journey" to improve efficiency. GE was able to eliminate inefficiencies, cut down on downtime, and increase output thanks to the adoption of lean principles and the use of digital technologies.

Lean Digital collaboration has also had an effect on healthcare thanks to developments like telemedicine and remote patient monitoring. Access to care, costs, and patient outcomes have all been positively impacted by these technological advancements.

Expert consensus and examples of effective change in practise show that Lean Digital collaboration is here to stay as technology continues to transform businesses. It's a chance to foster a collective mindset that values rapid problem solving, creative thinking, and teamwork.

- **Learning the Lean Digital Philosophy**

The following highlights clarify this philosophy's major ideas:

1. Lean Digital transformation places an emphasis on finding and getting rid of inefficiencies, bottlenecks, and processes that don't provide value. Automation of processes, increased efficiency in resource utilisation, and decreased waste are just some of the benefits that can arise for businesses that use digital technologies.

2. The culture of continual improvement is encouraged by the Lean Digital mindset. It promotes the use of experimentation, feedback loops, and data-driven decision-making within organisations as a means of fostering innovation and improving processes, products, and services. Data may be collected and analysed in real time with the use of digital tools, allowing for iterative improvements to be made quickly.

3. The focus of a customer-centric digital transformation strategy is on the customer. Organisations may learn many things about their customers' habits, likes, and requirements through the use of digital tools like analytics, AI, and CRM systems. This paves the way for customised services, precise advertising, and the creation of products with the consumer in mind.

4. Lean Digital organisations are smooth and adaptable, able to quickly adjust to evolving market conditions. They use digital tools to facilitate interdisciplinary teamwork, decentralised decision-making, and iterative approaches to project management. This encourages flexibility, toughness, and the capacity to seize novel chances in the online world.

- **Experts' Views and Supporting Research**

Many experts believe that Lean Digital is becoming increasingly important in today's digital world, as the number of digital users continues to grow. The growth of digital users has been driven by the increasing availability of digital devices and the increasing use of the internet, which has made digital products and services more accessible to people around the world.

An expert in the field of Lean Digital is **Eric Ries**, author of The Lean Start-up. Ries argues that Lean Digital is particularly important in today's fast-paced digital world, where customers expect high-quality digital products and services that are delivered quickly and efficiently. He suggests that companies that adopt Lean Digital methodologies are more likely to be successful in today's digital marketplace, as they are able to create and deliver digital products and services that meet the needs of their customers.

Steve Blank, a Lean start-up counsellor and mentor, is another expert in the field of Lean Digital. Blank contends that Lean Digital is critical for firms seeking to compete in today's digital economy because it enables them to swiftly test and iterate on their digital products and services, as well as respond promptly to user input. He also claims that organisations who use Lean Digital approaches are more likely to succeed in today's fast-paced digital market because they can produce high-quality digital products and services swiftly and effectively.

There are several studies and research that show that the number of digital users will continue to increase in the future. For example, a recent study by the **Pew Research** Center found that the number of people who use the internet has grown dramatically in recent years, with the majority of people now using the internet regularly. The study found that nearly nine out of ten people in the United States now use the internet, and that the majority of people use the internet for activities such as emailing, searching for information, and shopping online.

Another study by the **United Nations** found that the number of people who use the internet is increasing rapidly around the world, particularly in developing countries. This suggests that the number of digital users will continue to grow in the future, as more and more people around the world gain access to digital devices and the internet.

This makes Lean Digital increasingly important, as companies need to be able to create and deliver high-quality digital products and services quickly and efficiently in order to meet the needs of their customers. Companies that adopt Lean Digital methodologies are more likely to be successful in today's digital marketplace, as they are able to create and deliver digital products and services that meet the needs of their customers, and respond quickly to customer feedback.

Key Takeaways

The rise of a new era in business operations is characterized by the adoption of lean and digitized approaches. Lean philosophy, which focuses on reducing waste, enhancing efficiency, and maximizing customer value, has proven to be successful in both physical and digital operations.

The benefits of lean extend beyond cost reduction and improved quality to include enhanced customer satisfaction and a more efficient workplace. As the number of digital users continues to grow, companies that embrace Lean Digital methodologies are more likely to succeed in today's digital marketplace by creating and delivering high-quality digital products and services quickly and efficiently, meeting the needs of their customers, and responding quickly to customer feedback.

1.5 Why Lean Digital Thinking Is The Biggest Lever?

Here's why "Lean Digital thinking" is the best tool for companies looking to make digital shifts that stick. By embracing new technology and adopting a lean attitude, businesses may unleash significant efficiency, leverage artificial intelligence (AI), reduce rising labour costs, and keep teams clear of uncertainty.

Improving efficiency and streamlining processes is mostly dependent on innovative technological developments. For instance, robotic process automation (RPA) and other automation techniques can streamline repetitive activities with minimal human participation, thereby maximising efficiency. Robotics and automation have been used by companies like Amazon to completely revamp their warehouse and fulfilment systems, resulting in massive savings and improvements in efficiency.

When it comes to the world of Lean Digital thinking, AI is another revolutionary concept. Using AI algorithms and machine learning, businesses are able to obtain actionable insights from massive amounts of data, leading to better decisions and a more satisfying customer experience. Companies like Netflix use AI-powered recommendation systems to tailor their users' experiences, which in turn boosts customer retention and loyalty.

Lean Digital thinking is becoming increasingly important as labour prices rise. Companies need to maximise resource utilisation and output as wages rise and competition for workers heats up. Lean inventory management, demand forecasting, and just-in-time production are just a few examples of how digital technology is enabling lean processes, which in turn reduce waste and buffer the effects of rising labour costs.

However, the introduction of new technology can cause confusion and slow growth without the correct thinking and attitude. Building a culture of lifelong education, teamwork, and flexibility is essential for any successful business. Aligning teams and ensuring a smooth transition to Lean Digital practises requires proper training, change management tactics, and clear communication.

In today's business environment, success frequently hinges on a company's ability to stay ahead of the competition by adapting and continually developing. Companies must adapt new ways of thinking and working to remain relevant as technology and digital transformation continue to play a bigger role in the corporate world. Lean Digital Thinking is one of the most successful ways to this problem.

Are you feeling overwhelmed by the fast-paced digital world and attempting to stay ahead of the competition? Do you find it difficult to discover an effective way to adapt and continually enhance your business? Do you want to reduce waste, boost efficiency, and promote continuous development in your digital goods and services?

If your answer is yes, then Lean Digital Thinking might be the solution for you.

1.5.1 What is Lean Digital Thinking?

Lean Digital Thinking is a unique management philosophy that combines the best of both worlds - traditional Lean principles and the latest digital technologies. It is a proven methodology that helps organizations streamline their processes, eliminate waste, and create digital products and services that are efficient, effective, and user-friendly.

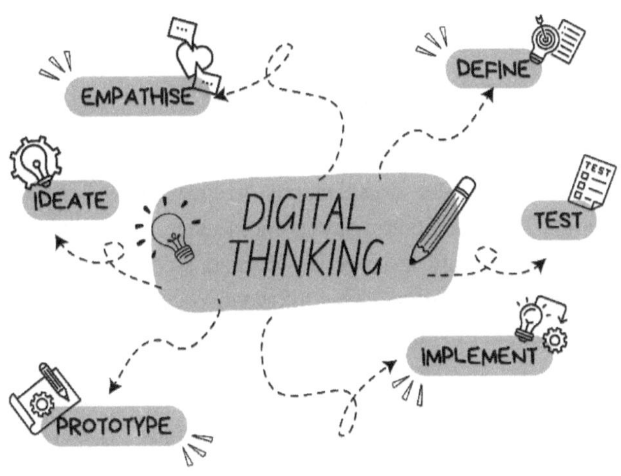

Figure 4: *Lean Digital Thinking*

By embracing the Lean Digital Thinking approach, companies can stay ahead of the competition and stay relevant in the constantly evolving digital world. They can create and deliver digital products and services that meet the needs and expectations of their customers, while continuously improving and adapting to new technologies.

1.5.2 Why is Lean Digital thinking the biggest lever?

1. Increased Efficiency and Productivity

Increased Efficiency and Productivity: The focus on streamlining processes and reducing waste in Lean Digital Thinking leads to increased efficiency and productivity. For example, by adopting this approach, a company in the healthcare sector could create digital tools that automate repetitive tasks, freeing up time for healthcare professionals to focus on more critical tasks. This increased efficiency leads to better patient outcomes, driving business growth and success.

2. Improved User Experience

Lean Digital Thinking takes a customer-centric approach to product design and development, resulting in a better user experience. For instance, a retail company that adopts this approach could create a mobile app that allows customers to easily search for products, compare prices and place orders. This improved user experience would lead to higher customer satisfaction, driving repeat business and customer loyalty.

3. Faster Time-to-Market

Emphasizing rapid iteration and continuous improvement, Lean Digital Thinking results in faster time-to-market for digital products and services. For example, a tech company that adopts this approach could release a minimum viable product, gather customer feedback, and quickly iterate to improve the product. This allows the company to stay ahead of the competition and meet the demands of an ever-evolving market.

4. Better Data Management

Lean Digital Thinking enables organizations to manage and analyze data more effectively, leading to better decision-making. For instance, a financial services company that adopts this approach could leverage big data analytics tools to gain insights into customer behaviour and preferences. This information could then be used to improve products and services, resulting in increased customer satisfaction and loyalty.

5. Increased Customer Satisfaction

By focusing on the user experience and streamlining processes, Lean Digital Thinking ultimately results in increased customer satisfaction. For example, a logistics company that adopts this approach could create a digital platform that allows customers to track shipments in real-time, reducing wait times and improving the overall customer experience. This increased customer satisfaction drives business growth and success.

6. Cost Savings

Lean Digital Thinking helps organizations reduce waste and increase efficiency, leading to cost savings. For instance, a manufacturing company that adopts this approach could streamline processes to reduce the costs associated with production, enabling it to invest in other areas of the business. This cost savings drives business growth and success in the long term.

7. Improved Employee Satisfaction

Lean Digital Thinking also improves employee satisfaction, as it encourages collaboration and creativity. For example, a marketing company that adopts this approach could bring together cross-functional teams to work on a project, encouraging employees to share knowledge and develop their skills. This increased job satisfaction and motivation drive business growth and success, as motivated employees are more likely to produce high-quality work and drive innovation.

1.5.3 Adopting Lean Digital thinking

Adopting Lean Digital Thinking can seem daunting, but it is a process that can be broken down into manageable steps. Here are some steps companies can take to adopt Lean Digital Thinking:

1. **Assess Current Processes**: The first step in adopting Lean Digital Thinking is to assess current processes and identify areas for improvement. This can be done

through a process analysis, where teams identify and eliminate waste, increase efficiency, and drive continuous improvement.

2. **Embrace a Customer Centric Approach**: Lean Digital Thinking prioritizes a customer-centric approach, so it is important for companies to put the customer at the center of their design and development process. This can be achieved by conducting customer research, gathering feedback, and continuously iterating based on customer needs and preferences.

3. **Encourage Collaboration and Cross-Functional Teams**: Lean Digital Thinking emphasizes collaboration and cross-functional teams, so companies should encourage their employees to work together in order to drive innovation and improve processes. This can be done by providing opportunities for team members to share their ideas and expertise, as well as by encouraging a culture of continuous learning and improvement.

4. **Invest in Digital Technologies:** In order to fully embrace Lean Digital Thinking, companies must invest in the latest digital technologies. This can include tools for data analysis, project management, and user experience design. By investing in these technologies, companies can streamline processes, reduce waste, and drive continuous improvement.

5. **Continuously Monitor and Iterate:** Finally, it is important for companies to continuously monitor and iterate their processes in order to stay ahead of the competition and meet the evolving needs of the market. This can be achieved by regularly conducting customer research, tracking key metrics, and continuously iterating based on customer feedback.

Key Takeaways

Lean Digital Thinking is the biggest lever for companies seeking to stay ahead of the competition and meet the evolving needs of the market. By streamlining processes, reducing waste, and putting the customer at the center of the design process, companies can create digital products and services that are more efficient, effective, and user-friendly. Additionally, by investing in the latest digital technologies and encouraging collaboration and cross-functional teams, companies can drive innovation and improve employee satisfaction, ultimately leading to business growth and success.

1.6 How A Successful Lean Digital Framework Works?

How to effectively implement and handle the challenges of digital transformation, as shown by the essential components of a Lean Digital framework. By learning these concepts, readers will have a solid foundation on which to launch their own successful, Lean Digital projects.

An organisation's goals must be aligned with the Lean Digital framework's vision and strategy for it to be successful. The process begins with a clear statement of objectives, followed by the selection of relevant KPIs and the establishment of achievable goals. This puts forth a plan for the process of adopting digital.

Working together across different teams and departments is essential for a successful Lean Digital implementation. In order to promote innovation and steady progress, it's important to eliminate barriers between departments and encourage open dialogue and teamwork. Organisations can streamline communication and the transfer of information by utilising digital tools and platforms.

Lean Digital frameworks rely heavily on agile and iterative approaches. Taking an iterative approach helps businesses respond rapidly to shifting client demands and market conditions. Teams may provide incremental value and quickly address feedback when large projects are broken down into smaller, more achievable jobs.

Decisions based on strong facts are crucial to the Lean Digital transformation process. The capacity of a corporation to draw conclusions, make decisions, and drive for continuous improvement is all dependent on its data analytics skills, which must be robust. The use of data in decision-making ensures that decisions are based on facts rather than speculation.

Adaptability and learning A effective Lean Digital framework fosters a culture of learning and transformation. Encourage staff to use emerging technology, gain new skills, and share knowledge to promote innovation and resilience. Businesses can therefore stay up with the ever-changing digital world.

1.6.1 Five focus areas

"Welcome to the Lean Digital Framework, where the customer is at the heart of every digital transformation effort. With a deep understanding of your customer's needs, desires, and behaviours, and a well-defined digital strategy that aligns with your business goals, you can succeed in today's competitive market.

Benchmarking against industry trends and best practices, investing in employee development, utilizing technology as a process enabler, and creating a sustainable game plan are the five key focus areas that we will explore.

Let's dive in and discover how to transform your organization digitally!"

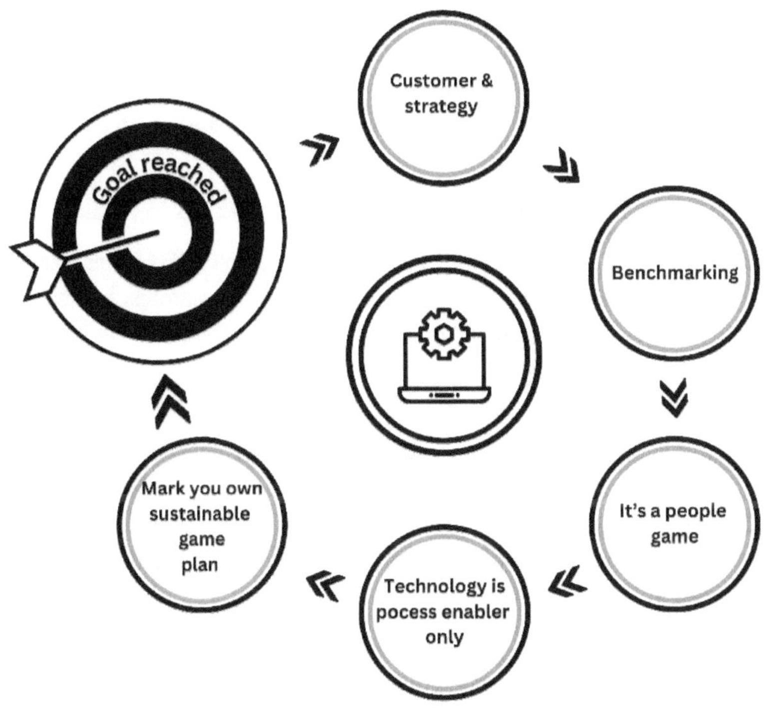

Figure 5: Five Focus Areas

FOCUS 1: CUSTOMER & STRATEGY

The first focus area in a successful Lean Digital Framework is the customer and strategy. The customer must be at the centre of any digital transformation effort, and a deep understanding of their needs, desires, and behaviors is essential. Organizations must conduct customer research, analyze customer data, and engage with customers through feedback loops to gain this understanding.

Once the organization has a solid understanding of the customer, they can then align its goals and objectives with the customer's needs. This requires a clear and well-defined digital strategy that aligns with the organization's overall business strategy. The digital strategy must take into account the organization's strengths, weaknesses, opportunities, and threats (SWOT analysis) and identify the key drivers of the business.

To ensure the digital strategy is effective, the organization must also be aware of what is happening in the world and learn from other organizations in similar industries or business contexts. This involves benchmarking against competitors, best practices, and market trends and keeping an eye on the latest technological advancements and their potential impact on the business. A good example of a company that focuses on customer needs is **Amazon**. Amazon's digital strategy is centered around its customer obsession, which drives everything they do. They constantly analyze customer data and feedback to improve their offerings and deliver an exceptional customer experience. This customer-centric approach has helped Amazon become one of the most successful companies in the world.

FOCUS 2: BENCHMARKING- UNDERSTANDING THE WORLD

The second focus area in a successful Lean Digital Framework is benchmarking and understanding what is happening in the world. Organizations must be aware of the latest market trends, best practices, and technological advancements in their industry to stay competitive and relevant.

Benchmarking against competitors, industry leaders, and best practices can provide valuable insights into what is working well and what can be improved. For example, organizations can compare their website design, customer experience, and online presence with their competitors to identify opportunities for improvement. This type of analysis can also help organizations stay ahead of industry trends and anticipate future developments.

A great example of a company that has excelled in this area is **Apple**. Apple's digital strategy is built on a deep understanding of their customers and the market. They continually innovate and set the standard for design and user experience, which has helped them maintain a loyal customer base and stay ahead of their competitors.

FOCUS 3: IT'S A PEOPLE GAME

The third focus area in a successful Lean Digital Framework is people. While technology plays a crucial role in digital transformation, it is the people within the organization who drive success. A strong and engaged workforce is critical to the success of any digital transformation effort.

To foster a culture of innovation and continuous improvement, organizations must create an environment that supports the change and encourages employees to embrace new ideas and technologies. This includes investing in training and development programs, hiring digital talent, and creating a digital-first mindset among employees.

Investing in the development of digital skills, both for existing employees and new hires, is essential to ensure the organization is equipped to navigate the ever-evolving digital landscape.

A great example of a company that has succeeded in this area is **Google**. Google invests heavily in employee development and encourages a culture of innovation and experimentation. This has helped them attract top talent and develop cutting-edge technologies that have transformed the industry.

FOCUS 4: TECHNOLOGY IS A PROCESS ENABLER

The fourth focus area in a successful Lean Digital Framework is technology as a process enabler. While technology is an important tool for digital transformation, it is not the sole driver of success. Technology must be used in a way that enables and supports the organization's goals, objectives, and processes.

One key aspect of utilizing technology as a process enabler is the integration of data and systems. Organizations must have the ability to collect, process, and analyze large amounts of data in order to make informed decisions. This requires the integration of data from multiple sources and the use of advanced analytical tools and techniques. By leveraging data and technology, organizations can gain valuable insights into customer behavior and preferences and use this information to drive business growth and improve customer satisfaction.

Another aspect of utilizing technology as a process enabler is automating manual processes. Automation can help organizations to streamline operations, reduce errors, and increase efficiency. This can result in cost savings, improved customer experiences, and a more agile and responsive organization.

A great example of a company that has excelled in this area is **Netflix**. Netflix uses technology to collect and analyze customer data and develop personalized recommendations. They have also automated many of their processes, such as content delivery and customer support, which has helped them become one of the world's most efficient and successful streaming services.

FOCUS 5: MAKE YOUR OWN SUSTAINABLE GAME PLAN

The final focus area in a successful Lean Digital Framework is creating a sustainable game plan. Digital transformation is an ongoing process, and organizations must continuously evaluate and improve their processes, systems, and strategies in order to achieve their desired outcomes.

One key aspect of creating a sustainable game plan is continuous improvement. Organizations must continuously evaluate their processes and systems and identify opportunities for improvement. This can be achieved through a variety of methods, such as customer feedback, data analysis, and benchmarking against industry leaders. By continuously improving their processes and systems, organizations can stay competitive and relevant in the rapidly changing digital landscape.

Another important aspect of creating a sustainable game plan is creating a culture of innovation and continuous improvement. Organizations must encourage employees to embrace new ideas, technologies, and processes and provide them with the resources and support they need to succeed. This can be achieved through employee training, development programs, and the creation of a supportive work environment.

Microsoft is an excellent example of a corporation that has achieved success in this field. Microsoft's digital transformation has been an ongoing process, with the company's products and services developing to suit changing consumer requirements and market trends. They have also invested in staff development and an innovative culture, which has allowed them to stay ahead of the curve and relevant in the business.

Key Takeaways

Successful Lean Digital frameworks prioritise the demands of their customers, simplify their operations, and use agile methods. If you want the best results, you need to work across departments and make decisions based on facts. Effective change management necessitates continuous learning as well as measuring and analysing performance. The framework necessitates an integrative approach and promotes a never-ending drive for betterment. The digital ecosystem is constantly changing, but by following these lessons, businesses can adapt to the new environment and thrive.

Chapter Summary

- At the beginning of the chapter, we look at the common belief that, in today's business world, digital technology implementation alone is sufficient to guarantee success. It stresses the importance of learning more about the Lean Digital methodology and how to put it to use.

- Next, we investigate why so many businesses have failed to succeed with their Lean Digital initiatives. Internal politics and competence gaps, such as a lack of leadership support and insufficient skills, are discussed, along with how they can impede the successful implementation of Lean Digital practises.

- Lean Digital is defined in this chapter as the integration of lean thinking with modern-day technological innovation. It discusses how Lean Digital promotes agility, efficiency, and customer-centricity to aid businesses in coping with the VUCA (volatile, uncertain, complex, and ambiguous) world.

- Also, we look at how Lean Digital has become an important factor in the current corporate environment. It looks at real-world instances of companies that have adopted Lean Digital practises and seen a rise in efficiency, creativity, and patron satisfaction as a result.

- It is argued that Lean Digital thinking is the greatest strategic lever available to businesses today. It illustrates how Lean Digital principles may help businesses cut costs, boost productivity, make better use of data, and foster a culture of constant innovation.

- In the final section of the chapter, we'll go through what makes a Lean Digital framework work. A customer-centric approach, data-driven decision-making, and a culture of experimentation and learning are all discussed, as is the significance of coordinating people, processes, and technology.

The chapter serves as an introduction to Lean Digital, delves into its difficulties and setbacks, emphasises its potential, and lays out the fundamental concepts and structure for adopting Lean Digital practises.

Key Questions for Readers 

- To what extent are your company's digital transformation activities in line with the company's long-term goals and strategies?

- What can be done to encourage teamwork and eliminate barriers between groups?

- Ask yourself this question: How might your company's digital endeavours benefit from an agile and iterative methodology?

- When making decisions based on data, what data analytics capabilities are necessary?

- How can you encourage a mindset of lifelong education and flexibility at work?

Part Two

Focus One: Customer & Strategy

Customer vs. CEOs vs. Leaders- Is it a Priority Gap?

"Lean Digital is not just about technology and processes; it's about placing the customer at the center of every decision and strategy. The gap between the priorities of the customer, the CEO, and the leaders must be closed for true digital transformation to occur."

~Sheryl Pattek, Chief Marketing Officer at Forrester Research

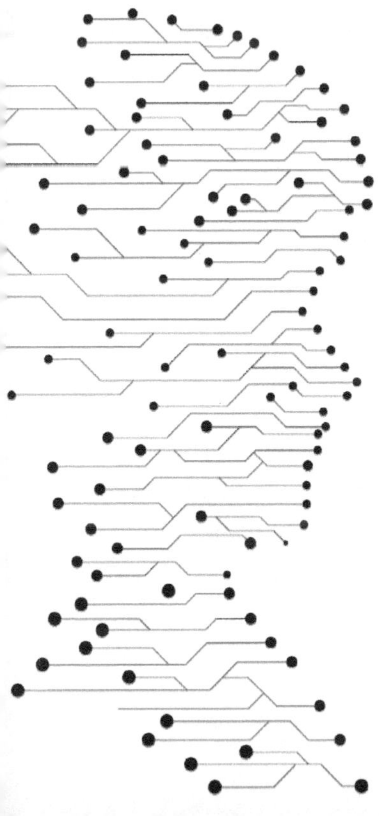

Customers are the heart and soul of any business. They are the reason why businesses exist, and meeting their needs and expectations is crucial to building a loyal customer base and sustaining a profitable enterprise. But as the world becomes increasingly digital and customers become more demanding and sophisticated, businesses must keep up with their evolving needs and preferences.

They want high-quality products and services, convenience, personalization, competitive pricing, trust, and excellent customer service. To meet these needs and stay ahead of the competition, businesses must adopt a Lean Digital approach to optimize their processes, reduce waste, and deliver value to customers.

Whether you're a small business owner or a marketing executive at a multinational corporation, read on to discover the insights and strategies you need to win over your customers and stay ahead of the competition.

This chapter will explore what customers want and how businesses can meet those needs.

Understanding and satisfactorily addressing customer desires is crucial to a company's success in the Lean Digital Transformation era. It's important to ask the proper questions and stay clear of typical problems if you want to obtain an insightful understanding of consumer requirements. In this chapter, we'll go into "What Customers Want" by outlining ten essential questions to ask clients as well as ten frequent mistakes businesses make when trying to gather client feedback. Best practises and current research were used as the basis for the offered information.

2.1.1 Ten Questions to Understand Customer Needs

1. What difficulties does your company or sector now face?
2. In what ways do you feel like your present approach or solution is falling short?
3. When conducting a Lean Digital transformation, what are the most important outcomes you hope to achieve?
4. How do you know when you've made it as a business?
5. Who exactly are your target consumers, and what do they anticipate from you?
6. Describe the perfect client interaction you can imagine.
7. What are the most important capabilities you need from a Lean Digital service?
8. Is it necessary to take into account any particular restrictions or limitations?
9. In what order would you list various features or specifications?
10. How do you foresee the adoption and rollout of a Lean Digital transformation?

2.1.2 Ten Common Mistakes Businesses Make When Trying to Understand Their Customers' Needs

1. One common mistake is assuming knowledge of consumer needs without first verifying or researching them.

2. Ignoring the needs of the client base in favour of concentrating on internal factors.

3. Not listening with empathy means not understanding what customers are going through.

4. Failing to ask in-depth questions that would reveal hidden interests and motivations.

5. Putting excessive importance on a single customer's opinion without first gathering feedback from a wider pool of customers.

6. Lack of a systematic method for recording and following up on client feedback.

7. Failing to adapt to the ever-evolving needs of your customers and the current situation of the market.

8. Reacting instead of anticipating customers' changing wants and needs.

9. Putting excessive trust in numbers while ignoring qualitative evidence.

10. Pretending that customers' wants and requirements are always the same.

One of the most important parts of Lean Digital transformation is getting to know your customers. In order to better understand their customers' wants and dislikes, businesses must ask the correct questions and avoid the usual mistakes. Ten important questions to ask your clients and ten common mistakes made by businesses have been outlined in this chapter. By applying these learnings to their Lean Digital transformation initiatives, businesses can boost customer happiness, accelerate innovation, and ensure long-term success.

2.1.3 Do you know - WHAT CUSTOMERS WANT?

1. Quality Products and Services

Customers expect businesses to provide high-quality products and services. Quality is no longer an option; it is a requirement. Customers are willing to pay a premium for quality, and businesses that do not deliver quality products and services risk losing customers to their competitors.

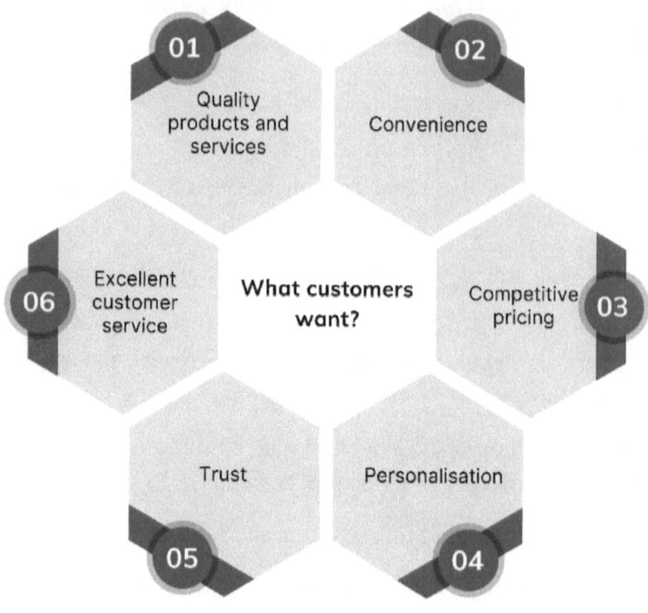

Figure 6: What Customers want?

To meet customers' expectations for quality products and services, businesses must adopt a Lean Digital approach that focuses on optimizing their processes and reducing waste. This requires a commitment to continuous improvement and a culture of excellence. Businesses must invest in quality control processes, use the best materials and technology, and ensure that their products and services meet or exceed customer expectations.

By adopting a Lean Digital approach, businesses can also use data to identify and address quality issues. For example, they can collect customer feedback and use it to improve their products and services. It can also use data to monitor its supply chain and identify areas where it can improve quality and reduce waste.

2. Convenience

Customers want convenience. They want to be able to buy products and services quickly and easily, without any hassle. This means providing multiple channels for customers to purchase products and services, such as online, mobile, and in-store.

Businesses need to implement a Lean Digital strategy that streamlines operations and reduces the number of engagements customers experience on their way to achieving their goals. For example, it can use digital tools to enable self-service options and provide multiple channels for customers to interact with its brand.

Businesses must also ensure that their products and services are easy to use and access. This requires simplifying processes and reducing friction points in the customer journey. Online ordering and smartphone check-in are two examples of how businesses can facilitate client interaction through self-service.

3. Competitive Pricing

Customers are price-sensitive. They want to get the best value for their money. This means that businesses must offer competitive pricing and value propositions.

Companies need to adopt a Lean Digital strategy that helps them cut costs and eliminate waste if they are to satisfy customers' expectations for competitive pricing. By streamlining its operations and optimizing its processes, businesses can reduce costs and offer competitive pricing.

Businesses can also differentiate themselves by offering unique value propositions, such as high-quality products at a lower price point or a better customer experience than their competitors. They can also offer promotions and discounts to incentivize customers to purchase its products and services.

4. Personalization

Customers want personalized experiences. They want to feel like businesses understand their needs and preferences and are catering to them. Personalization can take many forms, such as personalized product recommendations, personalized offers, and personalized content.

A Lean Digital strategy that makes use of data and technology to tailor the customer experience is essential if firms are to satisfy customers' increasing demand for personalised service. For example, they can collect customer behavior and preferences data and use it to make personalized product recommendations. They can also use customer data to personalize offers and promotions, such as sending a birthday discount or offering a loyalty reward.

Businesses can also use digital tools to provide customized content. For example, they can use personalization algorithms to recommend articles or videos based on a customer's interests. They can also use social media and email marketing to send personalized messages and offers to customers.

5. Trust

Customers want to trust the businesses they buy from. Trust is built through transparency, honesty, and integrity. Businesses must be transparent in their communications and interactions with customers, and they must deliver on their promises.

Trust can also be built through social proof, such as customer reviews and testimonials. Businesses can leverage customer reviews to build trust and credibility with potential customers.

6. Excellent Customer Service

Customers expect to receive excellent service. Customers want companies to solve their problems quickly and politely. This entails making available a variety of communication methods, such as phone, email, chat, and social media, to be used by customers.

Companies also need to invest in training for their customer service representatives so that they are well-informed, sympathetic, and quick. They need to be able to rapidly and efficiently fix problems for customers.

2.1.4 Why Understanding Customer Needs and Expectations are Important?

Understanding customer needs and expectations are crucial for creating value for the customer while eliminating waste and inefficiencies. By gathering feedback and data from customers, businesses can identify areas where they can optimize processes and eliminate non-value-adding activities. This can help businesses streamline its operations and improve the customer experience, leading to increased customer satisfaction and loyalty.

Moreover, understanding customer needs and expectations can help businesses develop a Lean Digital strategy that focuses on delivering value to the customer while minimizing waste. By identifying areas of improvement and optimizing processes, businesses can reduce costs and improve efficiency, which can lead to higher profits and competitive advantage.

In addition, in today's competitive digital market, it's crucial for companies to anticipate and meet the requirements of their customers. By leveraging technology and data analytics, businesses can gather insights into customer behavior and preferences, which can help them develop new products and services that meet the changing needs of their customers. This can help businesses stay ahead of the competition and remain relevant in the market.

Therefore, in a Lean Digital environment, understanding customer needs and expectations is crucial for driving value, innovation, and competitiveness. The consumer is the focus of a Lean Digital strategy that helps organisations optimise processes and cut down on waste by using data analytics and innovative technology.

2.1.5 How to Understand Customer Needs and Expectations?

Understanding customer needs and expectations is a crucial part of Lean Digital. Here are some ways businesses can gather customer feedback and insights: Here are a few examples:

1. Surveys and Feedback Forms

Surveys and feedback forms are simple and effective ways to gather customer feedback. Businesses can use online surveys or feedback forms to gather information about customer satisfaction, product or service quality, and areas where improvement is needed. It's important to keep surveys and feedback forms short and focused on increasing the likelihood of customers completing them.

2. Customer Interviews

Customer interviews are another effective way to gather customer feedback. Businesses can gain a deeper understanding of their needs and expectations by speaking directly with customers. Customer interviews can be conducted in person, over the phone, or through video conferencing.

3. Social Media Monitoring

Social media is a valuable tool for businesses to monitor customer feedback and engage with customers. By monitoring social media channels, businesses can identify areas where they are falling short and respond to customer complaints and inquiries in a timely manner. Social media can also be used to promote products and services and engage with customers in a more informal and personal way.

4. Website Analytics

Website analytics can provide valuable insights into customer behavior and preferences. By tracking website traffic and user behavior, businesses can identify areas where customers are spending the most time, what products or services they are interested in, and where they are dropping off. This information can be used to optimize the website and provide a better user experience.

5. Focus Groups

Focus groups involve a group of customers coming together to provide feedback on products or services. This method allows businesses to gather more detailed and specific feedback on their products or services. Focus groups can also help businesses gain insights into customer preferences and identify trends in the market.

6. Mystery Shopping

Mystery shopping involves hiring individuals to visit a business and act as customers. They can then provide feedback on their experience, including the quality of customer service, product knowledge, and overall experience. This method can provide businesses with an objective view of their customer experience.

7. Net Promoter Score

Net Promoter Score (NPS) is a simple tool that measures customer loyalty by asking customers how likely they are to recommend a business to others. This method can provide businesses with a quick and easy way to measure customer satisfaction and identify areas where improvement is needed.

2.1.6 The Role Of Digital Technology In Enhancing Customer Experience

Digital technology has transformed the way businesses interact with customers, providing them with a variety of tools to enhance the customer experience. Here are a few examples:

1. Personalization

Personalization is the process of tailoring products, services, and marketing messages to meet the specific needs of individual customers. With the help of Lean Digital technology, businesses can collect and analyze vast amounts of customer data, including browsing history, search queries, and purchase behavior. This data can then be used to create personalized experiences for each customer, such as personalized product recommendations or customized marketing messages.

For example, **Amazon**, the e-commerce giant, uses Lean Digital technology to personalize its customer experience. When a customer visits Amazon's website, the company analyzes their browsing and purchase history to recommend products that they are likely to be interested in. Amazon's recommendation engine is powered by machine learning algorithms, which continuously learn and improve based on customer feedback.

2. Streamlining Processes

One of the biggest frustrations for customers is having to wait in long lines or navigate confusing processes to get the service they need. By leveraging digital tools such as self-service kiosks, mobile apps, and chatbots, businesses can streamline processes and reduce wait times.

For example, **Starbucks**, the coffee chain, has implemented a mobile ordering system that allows customers to order and pay for their drinks before they arrive at the store. This system not only reduces wait times for customers but also allows Starbucks to collect data on customer preferences and behavior, which can be used to improve future customer experiences.

3. Improving Communication and Customer Service

Businesses may now interact with consumers in real time and offer fast support owing to digital technologies like chatbots and social media platforms.To give its consumers prompt service, **Delta Airlines**, for instance, has integrated a chatbot into its website and mobile app. The chatbot can assist with routine tasks like rebooking flights and answering inquiries about flight times and luggage policies.

4. Providing Customers with More Choice and Flexibility

With the help of digital tools such as online marketplaces and booking platforms, businesses can offer customers a wider range of products and services.

For example, **Airbnb**, the online booking platform, allows customers to book unique accommodations that they wouldn't find in traditional hotels. By leveraging Lean Digital technology, Airbnb has disrupted the traditional hospitality industry by providing customers with more choice and flexibility.

5. Providing Customers with a Seamless Omni-Channel Experience

Omni-channel is the process of providing customers with a consistent experience across all channels, including online, mobile, and in-store.

For example, **Nike**, the sports brand, has implemented an omni-channel strategy that allows customers to purchase products online, in-store, and even through social media platforms. By providing customers with a seamless experience across all channels, Nike has improved customer satisfaction and loyalty.

Key Takeaways

Lean Digital technology is vital in enhancing customer experience by providing more personalized, efficient, and flexible services. By utilizing digital tools and techniques, businesses can offer improved communication and customer service to their customers.

Lean Digital technology can streamline processes and enhance the efficiency of the business. This can lead to reduced wait times, faster transactions, and overall, better service to customers.

By using Lean Digital technology, businesses can provide customers with a seamless omni-channel experience. This means that customers can switch between channels, such as online, mobile, and in-store, without experiencing any inconsistencies in service.

2.2 What Investors Expect from Any Organization?

In today's business landscape, it's essential for organizations to understand both what their customers want and what their investors expect. Investors are the backbone of any organization. They provide the necessary capital for the business to function, grow, and achieve its goals. Investors have certain expectations from any organization that they invest in. Investors expect a lean organization that is efficient and effective in utilizing capital and resources to achieve its goals. They expect a clear and concise business plan that outlines the organization's value proposition and competitive advantage.

In addition, investors expect an organization to have a clear vision that is aligned with the needs of its customers and stakeholders. This requires effective leadership that can communicate and execute the vision, as well as a culture of continuous improvement and innovation.

Furthermore, consistent financial performance is essential for investors as it provides a measure of the organization's ability to generate returns on its investments. This requires a lean approach to financial management, including regular monitoring of key performance indicators, timely reporting, and proactive risk management.

Organisations frequently seek outside funding and investment to support their Lean Digital Transformation efforts. To attract and secure finance for these transformation activities, it is essential to understand what investors demand. This chapter will explore the issue of "What Investors Want" by offering ten central questions that may be correlated with investors in order to better comprehend their anticipations. We'll also go through the top ten errors that businesses make while trying to satisfy their investors. The data provided is founded on established standards and current studies.

2.2.1 Ten Questions for Assessing Investor Expectations

1. Why are you investing and how much do you want to make?

2. How can you figure out if a digital transformation project is worth the risk and how much development it could bring?

3. How long do you expect it to take until you see a profit?

4. When it comes to making decisions and keeping an eye on developments, how do you want to be involved?

5. When deciding which digital transformation projects to fund, what factors do you consider?

6. If you make a financial commitment to learn digital transformation, how do you evaluate its effectiveness?

7. What kind of transparency and reporting do you want from the companies you back?

8. What are your thoughts on maximising both immediate profit and long-term strategic value?

9. Investing in digital transformation initiatives, what are your ideas on their scalability and sustainability?

10. When it comes to creating value and gaining an edge in the marketplace, how important do you think innovation and technology are?

2.2.2 Ten Mistakes Companies Make While Capturing Investor Needs

1. Treating investors' expectations as though they were all the same rather than taking their preferences into account

2. Having an over-reliance on financial issues while ignoring risk management and strategy alignment.

3. Thirdly, not researching potential investors enough to fully understand their investment criteria and preferences.

4. Setting unachievable expectations by inflating or ignoring potential returns, resulting in distrust.

5. Failing to effectively communicate the benefits and competitive advantages of the company's digital transformation efforts.

6. Failing to keep people adequately and in a timely manner informed about how things are going with current projects.

7. Failing to take investor opinion into account while making decisions or adjusting strategy.

8. Not realising the value of maintaining relationships with investors after the first round of fundraising has closed.

9. Failing to accommodate investor needs and interests in setting organisational priorities.

10. Ignoring the long-term strategic consequences of investor partnerships in favour of short-term financial benefits.

2.2.3 Overview of Investor Expectations

Investors expect a lot from a Lean Digital organization as they seek to maximize its return on investment and minimize its risk. Here are some of the key things that investors expect from any Lean Digital organization:

1. Agile Development

Investors expect that the organization will use agile development methodologies to quickly iterate and improve its digital products and services. This approach allows the organization to respond to changing customer needs and market conditions quickly without incurring significant costs or delays.

2. Continuous Improvement

Investors expect that the organization will continuously improve its digital capabilities to stay ahead of the competition. This includes investing in new technologies, processes, and people, as well as constantly seeking feedback from customers and employees to identify areas for improvement.

3. Data-Driven Decision Making

Investors expect that the organization will use data to make informed decisions about its digital strategy. This includes gathering and analyzing data about customer behavior, market trends, and industry best practices, as well as using data to measure the effectiveness of its digital initiatives.

4. Customer Focus

Investors expect that the organization will prioritize the needs of its customers in its digital strategy. This includes understanding customer pain points, designing user-friendly digital experiences, and providing excellent customer service and support.

5. Lean Operations

Investors expect that the organization will run lean operations to reduce waste and improve efficiency. This includes using automation, outsourcing, and other technologies to streamline processes and reduce costs, as well as focusing on continuous improvement to eliminate inefficiencies and improve quality.

6. Strong Leadership

Investors expect that the organization will have strong leadership that can drive the digital transformation agenda forward. This includes setting a clear vision and strategy, communicating effectively with stakeholders, and empowering employees to take ownership of its digital initiatives.

7. Risk Management

Investors expect that the organization will have robust risk management processes in place to mitigate any potential risks associated with its digital initiatives. This includes identifying and assessing risks, implementing controls to manage risks, and monitoring and reporting on risks to key stakeholders.

8. Financial Performance

Investors expect that the organization will deliver strong financial performance as a result of its digital initiatives. This includes generating revenue growth, improving profitability, and achieving a strong return on investment.

9. Innovation

Investors expect that the organization will be innovative in its approach to digital transformation, exploring new technologies and ways of working to stay ahead of the competition. This includes fostering a culture of experimentation and learning and encouraging employees to take risks and think creatively.

10. Sustainability

Investors expect that the organization will have a sustainable digital strategy that takes into account environmental, social, and governance (ESG) considerations. This includes minimizing its carbon footprint, promoting diversity and inclusion, and ensuring ethical and responsible use of data and technology.

In summary, investors expect a lot from any Lean Digital organization. They want to see a focus on agile development, continuous improvement, data-driven decision-making, customer focus, lean operations, strong leadership, risk management, financial performance, innovation, and sustainability. By meeting these expectations, organizations can attract and retain investors, build a strong digital brand, and achieve long-term success in the digital age.

2.2.4 Key Financial Metrics and Performance Indicators of Investors

Lean Digital objectives are to streamline workflows, automate tasks, and continuously improve operations to deliver value to customers while reducing costs.

Investors evaluate the success of Lean Digital initiatives through various financial metrics and performance indicators. These include:

Return on Investment (ROI): This metric measures the financial return on the investment made in Lean Digital initiatives. A higher ROI indicates that the investment has been successful in generating returns. To calculate ROI, investors divide the net profit generated by the investment by the total cost of the investment.

Cost savings: A primary objective of Lean Digital initiatives is to reduce costs by eliminating waste and improving efficiencies. Investors look for cost savings in terms of reduced labor costs, lower operational costs, and decreased inventory costs. Cost savings can also free up resources for further investment in the business.

Customer Satisfaction: Lean Digital initiatives should ultimately result in improved customer satisfaction through faster response times, better product quality, and more personalized service. Investors look for metrics such as Net Promoter Score (NPS) and customer retention rates to gauge customer satisfaction. Improving customer satisfaction can lead to increased revenue through repeat business and positive word-of-mouth marketing.

Revenue Growth: While Lean Digital initiatives focus on cost reduction, they should also contribute to revenue growth. This can be achieved through improved product and service offerings, increased market share, and expanded customer base. Revenue growth can be an indicator of the long-term success of Lean Digital initiatives.

Time-to-Market: Lean Digital initiatives should enable faster time-to-market for new products and services. This can be measured by the time it takes to develop and launch new products or services. Reducing time-to-market can lead to a competitive advantage in the marketplace.

Employee Productivity: Improved workflows and automation should result in increased employee productivity. Investors look for metrics such as employee satisfaction and output per employee to gauge the impact of Lean Digital initiatives on productivity. Improved employee productivity can lead to cost savings and increased revenue through increased output.

Innovation: Lean Digital initiatives can also contribute to innovation by enabling faster experimentation and iteration cycles. Investors look for metrics such as the number of patents filed and new product launches to gauge the impact of Lean Digital initiatives on innovation. Innovation can lead to new revenue streams and a competitive advantage in the marketplace.

Overall, investors look for a balance of cost savings and revenue growth while also ensuring that Lean Digital initiatives contribute to customer satisfaction, employee productivity, and innovation. Tracking these metrics over time can help evaluate the ongoing success of Lean Digital initiatives and make necessary adjustments to achieve optimal outcomes. A successful Lean Digital initiative can lead to a competitive advantage in the marketplace, increased revenue, and improved customer and employee satisfaction.

2.2.5 How Lean Digital Strategy Can Contribute To Investor Satisfaction?

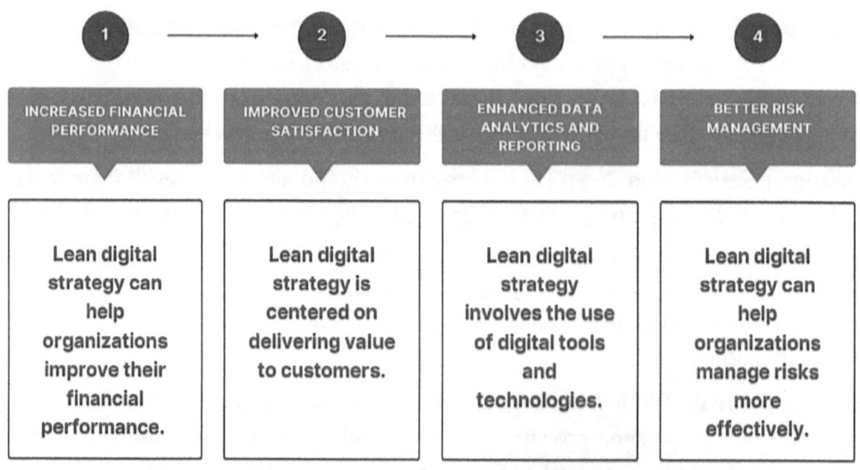

Figure 7: How Lean Digital Strategy Can Contribute To Investor Satisfaction?

A Lean Digital strategy is a business approach that aims to create more value for customers while reducing waste and increasing efficiency in operations. The Lean Digital strategy utilizes technology and digital tools to streamline processes, optimize resources, and improve organizational agility. Adopting a Lean Digital strategy can provide several benefits to organizations, including improving investor satisfaction in the following ways:

1. Increased Financial Performance

Lean Digital strategy can help organizations improve their financial performance. By streamlining operations, reducing waste, and improving efficiency, organizations can lower their operational costs and increase their profitability. Improved profitability can lead to higher revenue growth and better returns for investors, making the organization an attractive investment option.

Moreover, a Lean Digital strategy can help organizations stay ahead of their competition by enabling them to react quickly to market changes, adjust their strategies, and innovate faster. This agility can create new revenue streams and opportunities that contribute to the organization's financial performance and growth.

2. Improved Customer Satisfaction

Lean Digital strategy is centered on delivering value to customers. By adopting Lean Digital practices, organizations can enhance their customer experience by reducing response times, increasing product or service quality, and providing personalized offerings. Satisfied customers lead to improved customer loyalty, brand reputation, and revenue growth.

Investors look for organizations that have a strong customer base, a loyal customer following, and a solid reputation. Therefore, organizations that prioritize customer satisfaction through Lean Digital strategy can attract and retain investors who value customer-centricity.

3. Enhanced Data Analytics and Reporting

Lean Digital strategy involves the use of digital tools and technologies, such as data analytics and artificial intelligence, to streamline processes and optimize resources. These technologies provide organizations with better insights into their operations, customer behavior, market trends, and financial performance.

By leveraging data analytics and reporting, organizations can make data-driven decisions that can improve their financial performance, customer experience, and overall strategy. These insights can be shared with investors through regular and transparent reporting, which can improve investor confidence and satisfaction.

4. Better Risk Management

By using digital tools, organizations can identify and mitigate risks early, improve their response time, and minimize the impact of potential risks on their operations and financial performance.

Investors look for organizations that have a solid risk management plan in place to mitigate potential risks and protect their investments. Therefore, organizations that adopt the Lean Digital strategy can demonstrate their commitment to risk management and attract investors who value a well-managed investment portfolio.

Key Takeaways

A Lean Digital strategy can provide various benefits that contribute to investor satisfaction, such as Improving financial performance, enhancing customer satisfaction, strengthening data analytics and reporting, and enhancing risk management.

By implementing Lean Digital practices, organizations can create more value for its customer and operational costs and improve organizational agility.These benefits can make an organization a more attractive investment option for investors.

2.3 What Does the CEOs/CIOs Expect From Teams?

For any organization, meeting the expectations of both investors and its leadership team is crucial for long-term success. While investors expect strong financial performance and growth, the CEOs/CIOs is looking for a team that can help execute its vision for the company.

CEOs and CIOs play a crucial role in driving their organizations toward success. The CEOs, or Chief Executive Officers, is the highest-ranking executive in a company who is responsible for the overall strategy and direction of the organization. On the other hand, the CIOs, or Chief Information Officers, is responsible for managing the company's technology infrastructure and ensuring that it aligns with the company's goals and objectives.

Both the CEOs and CIOs have high expectations from their teams when it comes to Lean Digital strategy. They require their teams to be agile, efficient, and customer-focused. Leaders want their teams to have a deep understanding of their customers' needs, challenges, and aspirations. They expect their team to deliver products and services that cater to customers' expectations quickly and efficiently.

To meet these expectations, the team must be able to leverage digital technologies to automate processes, streamline operations, and improve the customer experience. It is also crucial for the team to understand how to use data analytics to gain insights into customer behavior and preferences. They must be able to use those insights to develop more effective marketing and sales strategies.

Moreover, CEOs and CIOs expect their teams to adapt to changing market conditions and to be able to innovate and stay ahead of the competition. They expect their team to identify emerging trends and technologies and to be able to leverage those trends and technologies to create new products and services. Teams need to be responsive to market shifts but also proactive in preparing for them.

Organisational success is heavily influenced by the goals and objectives set by the Chief Executive Officers (CEOs) and the Chief Information Officers (CIOs). CEOs and CIOs expectations for their teams' Lean Digital efforts are the primary emphasis of this chapter. It examines 7 typical problems seen during the implementation of Lean Digital initiatives and outlines 10 essential expectations. Best practises and current research were used as the basis for the offered information.

2.3.1 Ten Expectations CEOs and CIOs Have from Their Organization in Lean Digital Initiatives

1. CEOs and CIOs have clear expectations that their teams will connect Lean Digital projects with the company's long-term strategic goals and vision.

2. Prioritise digital projects that result in real business benefits, such as increased revenue, reduced expenses, and happier customers.

3. Third, focus on the consumer by making their desires and requirements the driving force behind all digital projects.

4. Commit to process optimisation, efficiency gains in operations, and new forms of innovation facilitated by digital transformation; these are the four pillars of our "continuous improvement" strategy.

5. Promote cross-departmental collaboration to ensure the smooth implementation of Lean Digital projects.

6. Adopt a data-driven approach to decision making, performance measurement, and the evaluation of digital initiatives.

7. Manage Change Well, Keeping Employees Involved, Trained, and Supported Throughout the Digital Transformation Process.

8. Adopt a culture of flexibility and adaptability to stay ahead of the curve as market dynamics, technological developments, and consumer expectations all undergo constant change.

9. Risk management number nine: find and eliminate threats to Lean Digital projects including security, privacy, and compliance.

10. Focus on Key Performance Indicators (KPIs) and Measurable Outcomes to Prove the Value of Lean Digital Projects.

2.3.2 Seven Challenges while Implementing Lean Digital Initiatives (CEOs/CIOs view point)

1. One of the most important aspects of digital transformation is creating a culture that is open to new ideas and willing to accept change.

2. Integrating new digital technologies and efforts with established legacy systems and processes.

3. Thirdly, we need to close the skills gap and empower the company with the digital expertise necessary for successful implementation.

4. Getting top management, individual departments, and the IT department all on the same page is a key part of the stakeholder alignment process.

5. Ensuring that Lean Digital initiatives can be implemented company-wide and kept going for the long haul.

6. Manage data quality, governance, and security to ensure accurate data for digital initiatives and decision-making.

7. Changes in organisational culture that encourage creativity, teamwork, and quick decision-making are crucial to a smooth Lean Digital Transformation.

2.3.3 Leadership's Expectations of its Teams

Leadership has high expectations of its teams when it comes to implementing a Lean Digital strategy. They expect their teams to be able to execute the company's strategy and deliver results. To meet these expectations, leaders require a well-trained and highly skilled workforce that is agile, efficient, and customer-focused.

Firstly, leadership expects its teams to have a deep understanding of the customer's needs and preferences. Teams must be able to leverage data analytics to gain insights into customer behavior, preferences, and feedback. With this understanding, teams can develop more effective marketing and sales strategies, resulting in an improved customer experience.

Secondly, leadership expects its teams to be agile in their operations, meaning they need to adapt quickly to changing market conditions. This requires the ability to respond rapidly to new challenges and opportunities. Teams must be able to optimize and streamline processes to reduce waste and inefficiencies and enhance the company's competitive position.

Thirdly, innovation is essential in implementing a Lean Digital strategy, and leadership expects its teams to be able to identify emerging trends and technologies and leverage them to create new products and services. Innovation requires a culture that fosters creativity and risk-taking, with leaders encouraging their teams to experiment, learn from failures, and continuously improve their processes.

Fourthly, collaboration is critical in implementing a Lean Digital strategy, and leadership expects its teams to be able to work together effectively, breaking down silos and sharing information and ideas freely. Strong relationships with customers and stakeholders must be established to facilitate a better understanding of its needs and preferences, enabling the organization to create products and services that resonate with its target audience.

Finally, leadership expects its teams to be well-versed in digital technology and to leverage it to automate processes, streamline operations, and improve the customer experience. Digital transformation has become a crucial element of modern business, and teams must be able to adopt and implement new technologies quickly and efficiently.

Key Takeaways

The expectations of a CEOs/CIOs from its team can vary depending on the organization's goals and objectives.

CEOs/CIOs expectations from its team vary depending on organizational goals and objectives.

Common expectations include commitment, dedication, and collaboration to achieve company goals.

Teams are expected to be innovative, adaptable, and able to work in a fast-paced environment.

Strong communication skills, being results-oriented, and making data-driven decisions are also expected.

Meeting and exceeding expectations can help earn the trust and respect of the CEOs/CIOs and drive organizational success.

2.4 What Do Other Leaders in The Organization Think?

To successfully implement a Lean Digital strategy, it is important to understand the perspectives of other leaders in the organization. Leaders may have different priorities, objectives, and concerns, which may influence their perceptions of the strategy. Therefore, it is crucial to engage in open and honest dialogue with other leaders to understand their viewpoints and identify areas of alignment and potential conflict.

Leaders from different functional areas, such as operations, IT, marketing, sales, and finance, may have different opinions on how to approach Lean Digital. For instance, operations leaders may be more focused on process efficiency and cost reduction, while marketing leaders may be more focused on customer acquisition and retention. Therefore, it is important to identify common goals and values that can be shared across different functions, such as customer satisfaction, innovation, and agility.

Moreover, it is important to involve other leaders in the strategy development process to ensure their buy-in and ownership. By involving leaders from different functional areas, it is possible to identify potential obstacles and opportunities early on and develop a more comprehensive and integrated strategy that addresses the needs of different stakeholders. Leaders can also play a key role in communicating and promoting the strategy to their teams and ensuring that the strategy is aligned with the overall vision and mission of the organization.

In this chapter, we'll look into the gap between top-level management and the rest of the company when it comes to strategy and Lean Digital projects. We will explore seven key disconnects by using real-world examples to illuminate the varying viewpoints found within organisations. The data and analysis presented here are based on real-world examples and extensive research.

2.4.1 Seven Major Gaps between CEOs/CIOs and Employee Understanding related to Strategy and Lean Digital Initiatives:

1. Vision and Strategic Alignment:

While the CEOs and CIOs may have a crystal-clear picture of the organisation's digital transformation route, other leaders and workers may have trouble seeing how their efforts fit in. Inadequate alignment and disjointed effort may result from such a gap. The CEO wants to move towards an omnichannel customer experience, but intermediate management doesn't understand the steps needed to get there.

2. Communication and Clarity:

However, other executives and employees may feel disconnected and confused about the general direction, despite the CEOs and CIOs assurances that the channels are effective in delivering the strategy and digital transformation goals.

For Example: A new analytics platform has been announced by the chief information officer (CIO), but its impact on day-to-day operations is unclear to supervisors at the front lines.

3. Digital Literacy and Skill Gap:

While CEOs and CIOs are aware of the significance of digital literacy and upskilling, other leaders and workers may lack the digital capabilities needed to actively participate in Lean Digital projects.

For Example: While the CEO stresses the importance of using data analytics in decision-making, some division heads may have difficulty comprehending and making use of the information at hand.

4. Change Management and Resilience:

It's possible that top-level executives will see the value in digital transformation and have the fortitude to see it through, while basic leaders and employees may be more resistant to change out of fear or ignorance.

Scenario: the CEO is pushing for a change to agile project management, but middle managers are reluctant to make the switch out of fear for their jobs.

5. Cross-Functional Collaboration:

Despite the necessity of cross-functional collaboration in achieving digital transformation goals, other executives and employees may find it difficult to work effectively together across departments and hierarchies, despite the constant emphasis on the issue from CEOs and CIOs.

To give an example, the CEO may urge the marketing and IT heads to work together on customer journey mapping, but this may not succeed due to misplaced goals and a lack of communication.

6. Performance Measurement and Accountability:

While CEOs and CIOs may have metrics and key performance indicators (KPIs) in place to gauge the success of digital initiatives, other leaders and employees may be confused as to how their actions affect these metrics, resulting in a lack of ownership and accountability.

Example: While the Chief Information Officer (CIO) may be aware of the importance of tracking website conversion rates, individual employees may be unaware of how their work affects these numbers and what they can do to improve them.

7. Cultural Transformation and Mindset Shift:

CEOs and CIOs may stress the importance of fostering a culture of innovation and agility, but other leaders and staff may find it difficult to make the mental change and adopt the new ways of working that are required.

The chief executive officer may advocate for trying new things and taking calculated risks, but not all department heads will step up and offer radical new ideas or question the status quo.

2.4.2 Importance of Cross-Functional Collaboration

Cross-functional collaboration is essential for successful Lean Digital implementation. Lean Digital requires a holistic approach that involves all parts of the organization, from customer insights to product development to delivery and support. Therefore, it is important to break down silos and foster collaboration among different functions, teams, and stakeholders.

Cross-functional collaboration can bring different perspectives and expertise to the table, which can lead to more innovative and effective solutions. By working together, teams can identify and solve problems faster, reduce duplication of effort, and improve communication and coordination. Collaboration can also create a sense of ownership and accountability as teams work towards a shared goal and celebrate successes together.

Moreover, cross-functional collaboration can help to create a culture of continuous improvement and learning. By sharing best practices, feedback, and insights, teams can learn from each other and adapt to changing customer needs and market trends. Collaboration can also promote a sense of empathy and understanding as teams develop a deeper appreciation for the challenges and opportunities faced by different functions.

To foster cross-functional collaboration, it is important to create opportunities for interaction and communication. This can be achieved through regular meetings, workshops, training sessions, and joint projects. It is also important to set clear expectations and goals and provide the necessary resources and support for collaboration. Finally, it is important to recognize and reward collaborative behaviors and outcomes, to reinforce the importance of cross-functional collaboration in the organization.

2.4.3 The Role of Communication and Transparency in Successful Strategy Implementation

Effective communication and transparency are critical components of successful strategy implementation, especially in the context of Lean Digital. As Lean Digital requires constant evaluation and improvement, it is important to establish clear communication channels and practices that enable timely, relevant, and transparent information exchange.

One of the primary roles of communication and transparency is to create a shared understanding of the strategy, goals, and expectations. This can be achieved through regular and open communication with all stakeholders, including employees, customers, partners, and investors. By communicating the rationale, benefits, and risks of the strategy, teams can develop a better understanding and commitment to the strategy. They can also align their efforts towards common goals and objectives and feel more empowered and engaged in the process.

Transparency is another crucial aspect of effective communication in Lean Digital implementation. By sharing ongoing feedback and updates on progress and results, teams can assess the effectiveness of the strategy and identify areas of improvement. Transparency can also create a sense of accountability and ownership, as teams are informed of their roles and responsibilities and are able to track their progress toward achieving the desired outcomes.

Furthermore, communication and transparency can help to foster a culture of innovation and continuous improvement. By encouraging feedback and ideas from all stakeholders, teams can identify new opportunities, learn from failures, and adapt to changing circumstances. Communication can also help to build trust and respect among stakeholders, as they feel that their opinions and contributions are valued and taken into consideration.

To achieve effective communication and transparency, it is important to establish clear and consistent messaging and provide multiple channels for information exchange. This can include regular team meetings, newsletters, progress reports, and feedback mechanisms. It is also important to ensure that communication is two-way and that all stakeholders have the opportunity to provide feedback and ask questions.

In addition, it is important to promote transparency by sharing both successes and challenges. This can help to build trust and respect among stakeholders, as they feel that they are being kept informed of both positive and negative outcomes. It can also help to create a culture of accountability, where teams are encouraged to take ownership of their actions and results and are not afraid to admit mistakes and learn from them.

Finally, it is important to recognize and reward open communication and transparency, to reinforce its importance in the organization. This can include acknowledging and celebrating successful outcomes, providing incentives for feedback and idea generation, and creating a safe and supportive environment for open communication and transparency.

Key Takeaways

Understanding the perspectives of other leaders is essential for effective decision-making and successful leadership.

Seeking input and feedback from colleagues can help leaders gain a broader understanding of the organization's strengths, weaknesses, and opportunities for growth.

Collaboration fosters a culture of teamwork and inclusivity, which can lead to improved performance, increased innovation, and a stronger overall organization.

Considering the viewpoints of other leaders is crucial for building strong relationships, driving positive change, and achieving success.

2.5 Is Lean & Digital Strategy Aligned with Company Strategy?

To determine if a Lean Digital strategy aligns with the company's overall strategy, it is essential to review its mission, vision, and values. These elements provide a clear picture of what the company wants to achieve, its direction, and the guiding principles that will help achieve its goals. By assessing the company's mission, vision, and values, it is possible to determine if the Lean Digital strategy is aligned with the overall company strategy.

For example, if the company's mission is to provide exceptional customer service, a Lean Digital strategy that focuses on enhancing the customer experience through the use of technology would be aligned with the company's overall strategy. On the other hand, if the company's mission is to be a low-cost provider, a Lean Digital strategy that focuses on reducing costs through the use of technology would be aligned with the company's overall strategy.

Business Example

In the past, there was a bustling city that was home to a firm known as TechVantage Solutions. Sarah Roberts, the company's CEO, decided it was time for a change after the company had been successful in the field of technology for a while. She was confident that the company might reach even higher heights if its employees adopted lean practises and made use of digital tools.

Sarah was aware that the company's general strategy, the lean strategy, and the digital strategy all needed to be in sync for the Lean Digital transformation to be effective. To address this crucial issue, she summoned a meeting of her top executives. Sarah started a conversation as they were all seated around the table.

She told the group, "Team, we have always been dedicated to providing outstanding value to our clients. It is time to integrate our lean and digital approaches into the larger goals of the firm. Every action we take should move us closer to our ultimate goal.

David, the CFO, posed a crucial query. "Sarah, how can we guarantee that our lean and digital strategies are in sync with the overall goals of our business?" How do we proceed?

Sarah grinned and described the future she saw. "To get our firm where it needs to go, we must first determine its long-term goals. These goals should be supported by our lean and digital strategies, which should in turn assist us in reaching our end goals. This requires coordinated effort and open lines of communication among all relevant teams.

Lisa, the CIO, elaborated, "To effectively align our strategies, we must engage employees at all levels." They need to know the big picture and how their role fits into it in terms of the company's strategy. This will give you a feeling of accomplishment and pride.

Sarah showed her approval by nodding her head. In a word, yes, Lisa. We need to encourage a mindset of constant development and creativity. The goals of our lean projects are to reduce inefficiencies and improve productivity, while the goals of our digital initiatives are to use technology to enrich our clients' offerings and push them towards operational excellence. Alignment isn't only about strategies, as the team realised as they brainstormed; it's also about mindset and behaviour. They realised the value of eliminating barriers, encouraging teamwork, and giving employees the autonomy they needed to accept change.

Throughout the process of transformation, TechVantage Solutions looked to professionals in the field for advice. They were encouraged by reading books like "The Lean Startup" by Eric Ries, which discussed lean concepts and digital innovation. They also read HBR pieces like "Digital Transformation: A Roadmap for Billion-Dollar Organisations" to learn more about how to coordinate digital tactics with overarching business goals.

TechVantage Solutions was able to successfully integrate lean and digital practises into its overall strategy thanks to the firm's dogged dedication to the task. The end result was improved operational efficiency, satisfied customers, and a more competitive position in the market.

2.5.1 Importance of Aligning Lean Digital Strategy with Overall Company Strategy

Aligning a Lean Digital strategy with the company's overall strategy is critical for several reasons. **First,** it ensures digital initiatives align with the company's goals and objectives. This alignment increases the chances of success because it ensures that resources are focused on achieving the company's most critical priorities.

Second, aligning the Lean Digital strategy with the overall company strategy provides clarity and direction to the organization. It enables employees to understand how their work contributes to the company's overall goals, creating a sense of purpose and motivation. This clarity and direction also make it easier for the organization to identify opportunities for improvement and make data-driven decisions.

Third, aligning the Lean Digital strategy with the overall company strategy promotes organizational agility. It enables the company to respond quickly to changing market conditions and customer needs, increasing its ability to stay ahead of the competition.

2.5.2 Assessing Company Goals and Priorities

It is essential to assess the company's goals and priorities to align a Lean Digital strategy with the overall company strategy. This assessment involves identifying the company's most critical business objectives and determining how digital initiatives can support these objectives.

One way to assess company goals and priorities is to conduct a SWOT analysis. A SWOT analysis examines the company's strengths, weaknesses, opportunities, and threats, providing insights into the company's internal and external environment. This analysis can help identify areas where digital initiatives can have the most significant impact and where the company is most vulnerable to disruption.

Another way to assess company goals and priorities is to review customer feedback and behavior. Understanding customer needs and preferences is critical to developing a Lean Digital strategy that enhances the customer experience. Customer feedback can also provide insights into areas where the company's digital initiatives are falling short and where improvements are needed.

While aligning a Lean Digital strategy with the overall company strategy can provide significant benefits, there are also potential risks and challenges that companies should be aware of.

One of the most significant risks is the potential for misalignment. Misalignment can occur when digital initiatives are not closely aligned with the company's most critical priorities. This misalignment can result in wasted resources and a lack of impact on the company's overall performance. Therefore, ensuring that all digital initiatives align with the company's goals and objectives is essential.

Another challenge that companies may face when aligning their Lean Digital strategy with the overall company strategy is the potential for resistance to change. Digital transformation requires a significant shift in mindset and culture, which can be challenging for some employees to embrace. Resistance to change can slow down the implementation of digital initiatives and make it difficult for companies to achieve their objectives.

Furthermore, some companies may struggle with the high costs associated with implementing a Lean Digital strategy. Developing and implementing a comprehensive digital strategy requires significant investments in technology, staff training, and infrastructure. This cost can be a significant challenge for some companies, especially smaller ones that may have limited resources.

Another challenge that companies may face is the potential for a lack of technological expertise within their workforce. To implement a successful Lean Digital strategy, companies need to have employees who are highly skilled in using digital tools and platforms. However, finding and retaining this talent can be challenging, especially in highly competitive industries.

Finally, cybersecurity risks should also be considered when implementing a Lean Digital strategy. As companies become more reliant on digital technologies, the risk of cyber-attacks increases. Therefore, companies need to ensure that their digital infrastructure is secure and that they have robust cybersecurity measures in place to protect against potential breaches.

To mitigate these risks and challenges, companies should develop a comprehensive digital strategy that addresses its most critical priorities and aligns with its overall business strategy. The strategy should also include plans to address potential resistance to change and provide adequate resources for staff training and technology investments. Additionally, companies should implement robust cybersecurity measures to protect against potential cyber-attacks.

Key Takeaways

Aligning a lean and digital strategy with a company's overall strategy is crucial to success.

Incorporating Lean Digital practices can streamline processes, reduce costs, and increase efficiency.

Aligning the Lean Digital strategy with the company's broader strategy ensures that efforts are working toward the same goals and objectives.

A well-aligned Lean Digital strategy can improve financial performance, enhance customer satisfaction, and better risk management.

Lean Digital practices are a powerful tool for driving growth and success in today's rapidly changing business landscape.

In the digital age, Lean has evolved to encompass a mindset of continuous improvement and agility, where companies seek to identify and eliminate inefficiencies in their processes and operations. A Lean approach to digital transformation involves aligning digital tools and strategies with the company's overall goals and values and constantly evaluating and adapting to changing customer needs.

However, many organizations fail to realize the full potential of their digital initiatives, despite investing significant time and resources. The biggest myth in this regard is that digital can win without a lean mindset. This myth needs to be debunked, as a lean approach is essential for digital success. In this article, we will explore why digital cannot win without a lean mindset and provide examples of where digital initiatives have failed without lean thinking and succeeded with a lean approach.

Digital initiatives are often viewed as a panacea for all business problems. However, without a lean mindset, these initiatives can fail to deliver the intended results. Lean thinking involves optimizing processes by eliminating waste and continuously improving the value delivered to customers. Applying lean principles to digital initiatives is crucial to achieving success.

One area where digital initiatives can fail **without a lean mindset is software development.** In traditional software development, there is often a long cycle time from idea to production, with little feedback along the way. This can lead to wasted time and resources on features that do not provide value to customers. A lean approach to software development involves shortening the cycle time by releasing small, iterative updates and gathering customer feedback to inform further development. This approach ensures that the software being developed is meeting the needs of the customers, which leads to greater customer satisfaction and a better return on investment.

One example of a company that failed to apply lean thinking to its digital initiatives is **Blockbuster**. Blockbuster was a dominant force in the video rental industry, but the company failed to adapt to the digital age. When Netflix emerged as a competitor, Blockbuster focused on building a digital platform that would rival Netflix's offering. However, Blockbuster's digital platform was bloated and slow, with a confusing user interface. The company failed to recognize the importance of lean thinking in software development, which led to a subpar product that did not meet the needs of its customers. Blockbuster ultimately filed for bankruptcy in 2010.

Another main reason why digital fails **without a Lean approach is the failure to change underlying processes to fit the digital tool.** For example, a company might invest in a new digital platform for project management but fail to modify its existing processes to fit the tool. This can result in inefficiencies and wasted resources as employees struggle to adapt to the new system or continue to use old methods alongside the new one. In such cases, the digital tool becomes a burden rather than a solution, and the promised benefits of improved productivity and efficiency are not realized.

Another reason why digital fails **without a Lean approach is the lack of integration between different digital platforms.** In today's business environment, companies often use multiple digital tools to manage different aspects of their operations, from sales and marketing to logistics and supply chain management. However, if these tools are not integrated properly, data can become siloed, and communication can break down, leading to lost productivity and missed opportunities. For example, a company might use one platform for customer relationship management and another for sales, but if these two platforms are not integrated, customer information might not be up-to-date or accurate, leading to missed sales opportunities and frustrated customers.

Furthermore, digital transformation without a **Lean approach can lead to a lack of focus on customer needs**. In a rush to adopt new technologies and stay ahead of competitors, companies may lose sight of their customer's current needs and preferences. They might invest in flashy new digital tools without considering whether these tools actually add value for their customers, or whether there are simpler, more effective solutions available. In such cases, the company's digital transformation becomes a vanity project rather than a strategic investment, and the promised benefits of improved customer experience and loyalty are not realized.

Finally, digital transformation **without a Lean approach can lead to a lack of employee engagement and ownership.** When companies introduce new digital tools without consulting their employees or involving them in the process, employees may feel disengaged or resentful towards the new system. They may see it as a top-down imposition rather than a solution that benefits them and the company as a whole. This lack of engagement can lead to a lack of ownership and responsibility, and employees may not feel motivated to use the new tool to its full potential or provide feedback for improvement.

To illustrate these points, let us consider a few examples of digital transformation failures due to a lack of a Lean approach. One example is a multinational retailer that invested heavily in a new e-commerce platform to compete with online giants like Amazon. However, the company failed to integrate this platform with its existing systems for inventory management and logistics. As a result, customers experienced delays and cancellations, and the company lost sales and reputation. By neglecting to take a Lean approach and align its digital tools with its overall goals and processes, the company missed an opportunity to improve its operations and customer experience.

Another example is a software development company that adopted a new project management tool to improve productivity and collaboration. However, it did not take the time to train its employees on how to use the tool effectively, or to modify its existing processes to fit the new system. As a result, employees continued to use old methods alongside the new tool, resulting in confusion and inefficiencies. This lack of focus on process improvement and employee engagement ultimately hindered the company's ability to reap the benefits of the new tool.

A third example is a healthcare provider that invested in a new electronic medical records system to improve patient care and streamline operations. However, the company did not take a Lean approach to the implementation, and employees were not consulted or trained properly on the new system. As a result, employees struggled to adapt to the new system, leading to increased frustration and errors in patient care. This lack of focus on employee engagement and process improvement ultimately hindered the company's ability to achieve its goals of improved patient care and operational efficiency.

In all of these examples, the failure to take a Lean approach to digital transformation led to missed opportunities and wasted resources. By neglecting to align digital tools with overall goals and values, modify processes to fit the new tools, integrate different digital platforms, focus on customer needs, and engage employees in the process, these companies failed to achieve the promised benefits of improved productivity, efficiency, and customer experience.

2.6.1 Examples of Successful Lean Digital Strategies

Successful digital strategies are those that are developed with a lean mindset. Three examples of companies that have adopted a lean mindset in their digital strategy implementation and achieved significant success are Amazon, Spotify, and Airbnb.

1. Toyota:

Toyota uses digital technologies to make its lean production processes better. By using IoT and advanced analytics, Toyota improves production speed, cuts down on waste, and makes sure that things are always getting better.

2. Amazon:

Amazon uses digital technologies to analyse data in real time and improve the efficiency of its supply chain. Amazon cuts down on lead times, makes the best use of inventory, and improves the general efficiency of the supply chain by using predictive analytics and automation.

3. Spotify:

A Plan Agile methods are used by Spotify to make software development lean and effective. Scrum and Kanban are examples of agile principles that help Spotify adjust quickly to changing needs, release features in small chunks, and encourage continuous improvement.

4. Microsoft:

Microsoft uses Lean principles to make its IT processes more efficient.

Lean IT techniques help Microsoft make processes more efficient, cut down on waste, and provide high-quality IT services.

5. GE:

To improve its standard lean manufacturing, General Electric is going through a digital transformation. GE improves processes, allows predictive maintenance, and adds value-added services by using IoT, data analytics, and machine learning.

6. Lean Six Sigma in Health Care:

A Plan Lean Six Sigma is used by healthcare organisations to improve care for patients and make operations run more smoothly. Lean methodologies are used to improve healthcare service overall, streamline processes, and cut down on wait times.

7. Lean construction practices:

Construction companies use digital technologies to improve lean construction practices. Building Information Modelling (BIM) and other digital tools are used to make planning projects better, cut down on waste, and make teamwork better.

8. Lean UX in Digital Product Design:

Companies use the ideas behind Lean UX to make digital products that are lean and work well. Rapid prototyping, user testing, and iterative design cycles make it easy to respond quickly to feedback from users, which makes sure that goods are easy for them to use.

9. Netflix:

Netflix uses data analytics to make smart choices about how to create and serve content. Algorithms look at how users behave to make personalised content suggestions, improve the library of content, and guide data-driven strategies.

10. Coca-Cola:

Coca-Cola's digital marketing tactics are flexible because they use Lean principles. Agile marketing techniques help Coca-Cola adapt quickly to changes in the market, make campaigns more effective, and get customers more involved.

11. Airbnb:

Airbnb focused on unique and low-cost ways to get new users and keep old ones by using a lean approach to growth hacking. Airbnb's early success came from using platforms that were already out there, making referral programmes work better, and trying out different marketing methods.

12. Tesla:

Tesla uses a lean method to create new products, making small changes to electric cars and software patches over and over again. Tesla sends out over-the-air software updates that make functions and performance of vehicles better all the time.

13. Microsoft:

To improve service delivery and make processes more efficient, Microsoft uses lean concepts in its IT operations. Lean IT techniques help Microsoft cut down on waste, work more efficiently, and provide high-quality IT services.

14. Skanska:

Skanska uses lean building methods to make projects more efficient, cut costs, and make it easier for people to work together. The goal of lean construction is to get rid of waste, improve speed, and get the most value out of the building process.

15. Virginia Mason Medical Centre:

Virginia Mason uses lean concepts to improve the health of its patients and cut down on costs. Lean methodologies help streamline processes, get rid of waste, and improve customer satisfaction in healthcare delivery.

2.6.2 Importance of a Lean Mindset in Digital Strategy Implementation

A lean mindset is based on the ideas of continuous improvement, reducing waste, and putting the customer first. It has many real benefits that businesses can't ignore.

1. Understanding the Lean mentality:

A lean mentality is a way of thinking that started in manufacturing but is very useful in modern times. Some of the most important concepts are constant improvement, getting rid of waste, and always focusing on giving customers what they want. How businesses deal with problems and opportunities isn't just based on a set of norms; it's also a change in the way people think and act. A lean attitude focuses on getting rid of waste to make sure that resources like time and money are used effectively. With this practical method, businesses can invest in digital projects more wisely, avoiding wasteful costs and delays.

2. Being flexible in a digital world:

Technology, customer behaviour, and the way markets work all change quickly in the digital world. A lean approach gives businesses the flexibility they need to deal with this instability. It creates an environment where teams can quickly learn new things, try out new ideas, and react quickly to changes in the competitive scene.

3. Innovation through Iteration:

A key part of great digital strategies is innovation. A lean mindset encourages people to try new things and make changes over and over again. Teams are told to take calculated chances, learn from mistakes, and keep making processes better. This practical approach to innovation makes sure that digital goods and services stay on the cutting edge and useful in a world that is changing quickly.

4. Focus on the customer:

The focus on the customer shows how useful a lean mindset is in real life. When it comes to digital strategy, how well solutions meet customer goals is what counts. A lean mindset encourages regular feedback from customers, analysis of data, and small changes made over time. This makes sure that digital projects are not only technically sound but also useful to the people who will be using them.

5. Overcoming Challenges and making sure sustainability:

Receiving practical also means dealing with problems. A lean approach helps businesses find and get around problems in a planned way. Businesses can make sure that their digital projects will last in a world that is always changing by using feedback loops and changing their strategies based on real-time data.

Key Takeaways

It is a mistake to think that digital projects can guarantee success on their own without also embracing a lean approach. In order to successfully undergo digital transformation, it is necessary to adopt a "lean mindset," which emphasises efficiency, waste reduction, and continual development.

Inefficiencies, disconnected processes, and unrealized potential are all possible outcomes of adopting digital technology without first ensuring it is in line with lean principles. Sustainable success in today's fast-paced corporate environment requires a blend of lean concepts and digital methods.

- A lean mindset is crucial for companies that want to succeed in today's digital age.

- By prioritizing customer needs and continuous improvement, companies can optimize their digital strategy and differentiate themselves from their competitors. It also helps companies stay ahead of the competition by embracing a culture of innovation, using customer insights to develop relevant digital solutions, and allocating resources effectively.

- Digital transformation cannot be successful without a lean mindset.

- The digital landscape is constantly evolving, and companies need to embrace a culture of continuous improvement to stay competitive.

- Adopting lean principles can help businesses improve processes, enhance customer experience, and achieve better financial results.

- Digital transformation requires a holistic approach that goes beyond technology implementation.

- A lean mindset promotes a culture of experimentation, risk-taking, and continuous learning.

- Companies that embrace a lean approach to digital transformation are more likely to succeed in delivering value to customers, improving financial performance, and remaining competitive in the long run.

Key Questions for Readers

- How can businesses better grasp and satisfy the needs of their customers in the digital age, and what impact would this have on their bottom line?

- In today's technologically driven corporate landscape, what do you think are the most important characteristics that make an organisation appealing to investors, and how can businesses adjust their strategy to match these expectations?

- How can team members best contribute to the success of their organisation in light of the chief executive officer's and chief information officer's top priorities and concerns regarding digital transformation?

- When it comes to aligning lean and digital initiatives with the broader corporate strategy, what are some common perspectives and concerns that arise, and how can these perspectives be effectively addressed and resolved, taking into account the various leaders within an organisation?

- Please share your insights about the most common myths surrounding digital transformation and how a lean approach can help dispel these false beliefs and improve results.

- How do you think lean and digital strategies relate to one another, and how well do they match with the overall strategy of your own company? Do you perceive any particular opportunities or threats in this setting, and if so, how might they be exploited to the greatest effect?

Focus Two: Benchmarking- What's happening in the world?

Lean Digital - A Key Enabler, A Buzz or A Lipstick?

"Improvement usually means doing something that we have never done before."

~Shigeo Shingo

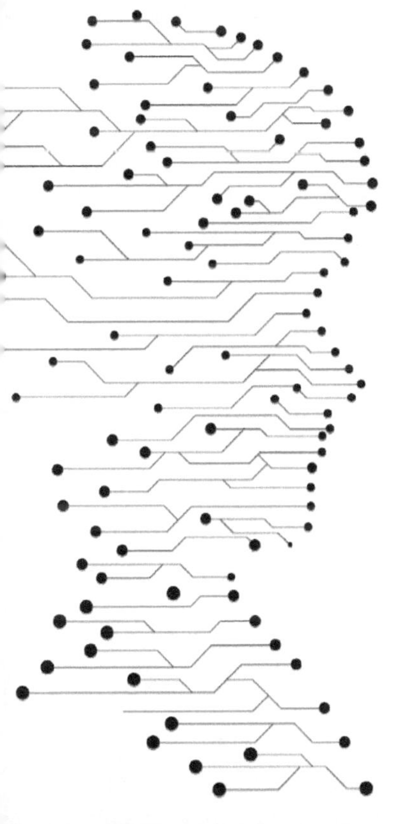

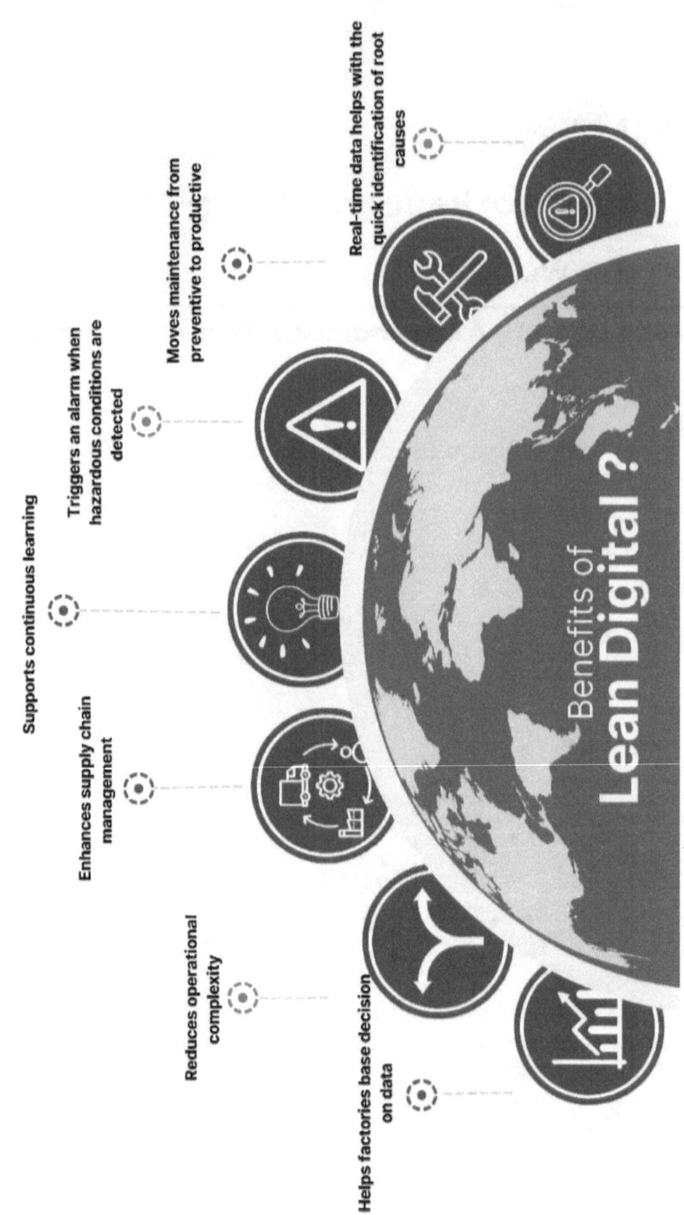

Figure 8: Benefits of Lean Digital?

GlobalTech, operating in a world where technology was developing rapidly, came to an agreement stage. Mark Thompson, CEO, saw that going digital was essential to the company's future success. But he also sensed widespread uncertainty about what digital transformation meant for the business among his leadership team and staff.

Mark called a meeting of his staff to discuss their worries. He realised that it would be unproductive if they regarded digital transformation as nothing more than a trend. He started off by explaining his plan.

"Team," Mark said to begin, "I know there's confusion about digital transformation, but I firmly believe it's the way to move our organisation forward.

To truly transform our business and the value we provide to our consumers, we need to do more than merely adopt new technologies.

Rachel, the CMO, put up her hand. Mark, the market's been buzzing about digital transformation for a while now. It's too much to take in. How do we identify the most obvious course of action?

Mark acknowledged her worry and nodded. "You're correct, Rachel. To begin, we must define what "digital transformation" means for our company. We have to take account of where we are now, figure out what's broken, and imagine how we can use technology to fix it.

David, the CIO, chimed in. "It's also important that we foster a robust digital culture here at the organisation." It's not just a matter of technical know-how but also of attitude and approach. We need to encourage employees to adapt to changing circumstances and look for ways to improve existing processes.

Mark followed in with an analogy in favour. Consider your digital transformation a trip. It's not something you get to do; rather, it's a journey. Taking this road will require us to be open-minded, flexible, and iterative.

The team approached leaders in the field for advice to help them along the way. Both "Digital Transformation in the Age of Disruption" by George Westerman and "The Four Pillars of Digital Transformation" by Brian Solis are required reading for this team. These resources were crucial in providing GlobalTech with the frameworks and examples it needed to develop its own digital transformation plan.

The team noticed improvements over time as they internalised the core principles of digital transformation. They used the latest technology to improve internal operations, delight customers, and fuel creativity. They promoted an environment where employees felt safe sharing ideas and taking risks in order to accelerate the company's digital transformation.

GlobalTech persisted and saw clearly how to turn chaos into order and a solution. They not only made it through the digital age, but they thrived as a result of their ability to adapt quickly and focus on their customers.

3.1.1 Let's get the Basics in Sync

Digital transformation is a term that has become ubiquitous in the business world in recent years. The rise of new technologies has allowed companies to innovate their processes, create new products, and streamline their operations, as illustrated above. The challenge is in understanding what digital transformation is and how to approach it strategically. In this chapter, we will explore the concept of digital transformation and how Lean Digital can be a key enabler in driving its success.

First, here are some key points to consider when it comes to digital transformation:

1. **Digital transformation is not just about technology:** While technology is certainly a key part of digital transformation, it's important to recognize that it's not the only focus. Digital transformation is about using technology to fundamentally transform the way organizations think about and approach their business processes, customer interactions, and employee experiences. It's about creating a more agile, innovative, and customer-centric organization. At its core, digital transformation is the integration of digital technologies into all areas of a business, which can involve a complete overhaul of the existing processes and systems and the adoption of new technologies that lead to significant changes in how businesses operate.

   Example: One company that has successfully implemented digital transformation is Burberry. They recognized that the luxury fashion industry was changing rapidly, and used technology to transform the way they interacted with customers. They developed a mobile app that allowed customers to browse and purchase products, as well as providing personalized recommendations based on their preferences.

2. **Digital transformation is a journey, not a destination**: Digital transformation is not a one-time project with a clear endpoint. It's a continuous process of innovation and improvement, driven by changing customer needs and new technologies. Organizations need to be prepared to adapt and evolve as the business landscape changes.

   Example: Starbucks is a company that has embraced digital transformation as a continuous journey. They have introduced mobile ordering and payment, loyalty programs, and personalized marketing campaigns based on customer data. They continue to experiment with new technologies, such as voice ordering through Alexa, to stay ahead of the competition.

3. **Digital transformation requires a culture of innovation:** Organizations must be willing to take risks and experiment with new ideas and technologies to achieve true digital transformation. This requires a culture of innovation and a willingness to embrace failure as a learning opportunity. Organizations must also be willing to challenge traditional ways of working and be open to new approaches.

   Example: Tesla is a company that has embraced a culture of innovation in order to disrupt the automotive industry. They have used technology to create electric cars that are both high-performing and environmentally friendly. They have also disrupted traditional sales models by selling their cars directly to consumers, rather than through dealerships.

4. **Digital transformation requires strong leadership:** Successful digital transformation requires strong leadership from the top down. Leaders must be willing to embrace change and lead their organizations through the transformation process. They must also be able to communicate the benefits of digital transformation to employees and customers.

   Example: Jeff Bezos, CEO of Amazon, is an example of a strong leader who has successfully led his organization through digital transformation. He has been willing to take risks and experiment with new technologies, such as the Amazon Echo and Alexa. He has also focused on creating a customer-centric organization, with a relentless focus on improving the customer experience.

5. **Digital transformation is not a one-size-fits-all solution:** Each organization has its own unique set of challenges, goals, and opportunities, and the digital transformation strategy should be tailored accordingly.

One way to approach digital transformation is to start with a clear understanding of the organization's current state, including its strengths, weaknesses, and areas for improvement.

Organizations that are slow to embrace digital transformation risk falling behind their competitors and losing market share. For example, Blockbuster Video, a once-thriving video rental chain, failed to adapt to the rise of digital streaming services like Netflix and ultimately filed for bankruptcy.

The Blockbuster example highlights the importance of staying ahead of technological trends and market changes. To avoid a similar fate, organizations need to constantly monitor emerging technologies and industry trends and adapt accordingly. This may require a significant investment in new technology and training, but the potential benefits in terms of increased competitiveness and market share can outweigh the costs.

Finally, digital transformation is not a one-time project but an ongoing process of continuous improvement and adaptation to changing market and technological trends.

Digital transformation is a journey, not a destination. It requires ongoing investment in technology, talent, and culture to stay ahead of the curve. To be successful, organizations need to embrace a mindset of continuous improvement and a willingness to adapt to changing market and technological trends. This requires a long-term commitment from leadership and a culture that values experimentation, agility, and continuous learning.

Key Takeaways

To truly transform an organisation into a digital business, you need a strategic and comprehensive strategy that integrates and optimises your IT infrastructure as well as your business processes and your people.

Lack of defined objectives, resistance to change, and insufficient digital skills and competencies all contribute to the mess that is digital transformation for many businesses.

Strong leadership, a clear vision, and good communication are essential for a successful digital transformation, as they will help to engage people and garner their support along the transformation path.

Key elements of digital transformation include data-driven decision-making and the use of new technologies like AI, cloud computing, and the Internet of Things (IoT).

3.2 Surprising Reasons for Lean and Digital Failure

Implementing Lean and digital transformations is never an easy task, and there are often many factors that contribute to the failure of such initiatives. While there are many reasons that are commonly cited for the failure of Lean and digital transformations, there are also some surprising reasons that can be overlooked. Here are some surprising reasons for failure.

1. Lack of Focus on People and Culture:

One of the most surprising reasons for the failure of Lean and digital transformations is the lack of focus on people and culture. Many organizations fail to realize that these initiatives are not just about implementing new processes or technology, but also about changing the way people work and think. Without proper attention to this aspect, the transformation may fail to take root and produce the expected results.

For instance, in the case of **Toyota**, which is often credited with popularizing the Lean methodology, the company's success was largely due to its focus on its employees and their involvement in the continuous improvement process. Toyota's emphasis on employee engagement and empowerment resulted in a culture of continuous improvement that enabled the company to become the world's largest automaker. Similarly, a focus on building a culture of innovation and agility is crucial for successful digital transformation.

2. Resistance to Change:

Another surprising reason for the failure of Lean and digital transformations is resistance to change. Even when the benefits of the initiative are apparent, people may still resist change due to various reasons like fear of the unknown, loss of control, and comfort with the status quo. This resistance can lead to a lack of buy-in from employees, which in turn can make it difficult to sustain the transformation.

For instance, **Blockbuster**, a leading video rental chain, failed to embrace digital transformation in its business model and continued to rely on its brick-and-mortar stores. This resistance to change ultimately led to the company's decline and bankruptcy when competitors like Netflix, which focused on digital innovation, took over the market.

3. Lack of Clarity in Objectives and Metrics:

Yet another surprising reason for the failure of Lean and digital transformations is the lack of clarity in objectives and metrics. Without clearly defined objectives and metrics, it can be difficult to determine whether the transformation is on track to achieve its intended outcomes. Additionally, without the right metrics, it can be difficult to measure progress and identify areas that need improvement.

For example, in the case of **Nokia**, the company's failure to establish clear objectives and metrics for its transition to digital technology resulted in the company's decline. Nokia failed to keep up with its competitors like Apple and Samsung, who established clear objectives and metrics for their digital transformation initiatives.

4. Lack of Cross-Functional Collaboration:

One equally important surprising reason for the failure of Lean and digital transformations is the lack of cross-functional collaboration. Many organizations fail to recognize that these initiatives require the participation and cooperation of multiple departments and functions. Without cross-functional collaboration, it can be difficult to ensure that everyone is on the same page and working towards the same goals.

For instance, in the case of **General Electric (GE)**, the company's failure to foster cross-functional collaboration during its digital transformation initiative led to its eventual downfall. The company's different divisions failed to work together effectively, resulting in a fragmented approach to digital transformation that ultimately failed to produce the desired results.

5. Overreliance on Technology:

Also, a surprising reason for the failure of Lean and digital transformations is overreliance on technology. While technology is certainly an important aspect of these initiatives, it's important not to overemphasize its importance at the expense of other factors like people, culture, and processes.

6. Lack of Clear Communication and Collaboration among Team Members:

Effective communication and collaboration are essential for the successful implementation of any transformational initiative. The leaders must ensure that all team members understand the goals and objectives of the initiative, and everyone is aligned towards achieving those goals. They should also encourage open communication channels and provide regular feedback to the team members to keep them motivated and engaged.

7. Lack of Training and Development Programs for Employees:

Many organizations fail to recognize the importance of training and development programs in building a culture of continuous improvement and innovation. These programs can help employees acquire the necessary skills and knowledge to implement new technologies and processes effectively. It is essential to invest in employee training and development programs to ensure that they can keep up with the rapid changes in the digital landscape and stay ahead of the competition.

8. Poor Data Quality:

Data is at the heart of digital transformation, and organizations that fail to prioritize data quality are likely to experience failure. Poor data quality can result in incorrect insights and decisions, leading to wasted resources and missed opportunities.

9. Insufficient Planning and Execution:

Insufficient planning and execution can also contribute to failure. Digital transformation is a complex process that requires careful planning and execution to succeed. Organizations that rush into implementation without proper planning are likely to encounter issues that could have been avoided.

10. Failure to Address Cybersecurity:

Digital transformation increases the organization's reliance on technology, making them more vulnerable to cyber threats. Failure to address cybersecurity risks can result in significant financial losses and damage to the organization's reputation.

Lastly, organizations must embrace a culture of experimentation and risk-taking to achieve successful Lean and Digital transformations. Many organizations are hesitant to take risks and try new approaches, which often leads to failure. Leaders must encourage experimentation and foster a culture of learning from failures. They should provide a safe environment where employees feel free to take risks, try new approaches, and learn from their mistakes. This culture of experimentation can help organizations stay innovative and agile in the rapidly changing digital landscape.

Key Takeaways

Organisational goals and objectives, as well as a defined strategy and roadmap for implementation, are essential for successful digital transformation.

For a company to undergo a successful digital transformation, it must undergo a broader cultural and organisational shift, which includes things like employee buy-in, training, and an openness to new ways of working.

One of the most typical causes of failed digital transformation is resistance to change and a lack of leadership support. The transformation activities of an organisation need to be driven and supported by capable leaders.

For digital transformation to be a success, there must be open lines of communication and teamwork. The success of any transformation depends on the participation and alignment of all stakeholders, including employees, customers, and partners.

To maintain consistency with organisational objectives and accommodate shifting market trends and technological developments, digital transformation programmes require constant monitoring, evaluation, and change. The ability to adapt quickly and easily is essential for a smooth digital transformation.

3.3 Excuses Leaders make while deploying Lean and Digital Transformation

Digital transformation and lean methodologies can transform an organization and boost its competitiveness, as shown in the graph below:

However, many organizations struggle to implement these changes effectively. Leaders often resist change, especially when they perceive it as a threat to their status quo. They may resort to excuses and rationalizations to avoid implementing digital transformation and lean practices. In this section, we will explore some of the excuses that leaders make when deploying lean and digital transformation and the reasons behind them.

1. "We don't have the budget for digital transformation."

One of the most common excuses leaders make when it comes to implementing digital transformation is the lack of budget. Organizations may believe that digital transformation requires significant financial resources, and they may not have the necessary funds to make the change.

However, digital transformation is not just about investing in new technologies. It is also about adopting a new mindset and culture that values innovation, experimentation, and collaboration. It is about finding new and creative ways to solve problems and serve customers. While some investment is necessary, organizations can start by developing a culture of innovation that encourages experimentation, creativity, and learning.

Case study: Amazon.com

Amazon.com is a prime example of an organization that has embraced digital transformation and developed a culture of innovation. Amazon started as an online bookstore, but it has since expanded into various other businesses, such as cloud computing, digital streaming, and artificial intelligence. Amazon's culture encourages experimentation and innovation, which has led to the development of new products and services that have disrupted industries and changed the way we live.

2. "We don't have resources to implement lean practices."

Organizations may believe that implementing lean practices requires significant financial resources, and they may not have the necessary funds to make the change.

However, lean practices are not just about reducing waste and increasing efficiency. They are also about developing a culture of continuous improvement, where everyone is involved in identifying and solving problems. Organizations can start by empowering their employees to make decisions, encouraging cross-functional collaboration, and creating a culture of continuous learning.

Case study: Toyota

Toyota is a prime example of an organization that has embraced lean practices and developed a culture of continuous improvement. Toyota's approach to lean is based on the principles of respect for people and continuous improvement. Toyota empowers its employees to make decisions, encourages cross-functional collaboration, and fosters a culture of continuous learning. This approach has enabled Toyota to achieve significant improvements in quality, efficiency, and customer satisfaction.

3. "Our industry is different, and lean/digital transformation doesn't apply to us."

Another common excuse that leaders make is that their industry is different, and lean/digital transformation does not apply to them. Organizations may believe that their industry is unique and that lean/digital transformation practices are not relevant to their business.

However, lean/digital transformation practices can be applied to any industry, regardless of its nature. It is about finding new and creative ways to solve problems and serve customers. By adopting a customer-centric approach and focusing on delivering value, organizations can transform their operations and improve their competitiveness.

Case study: Zara

Zara is a prime example of an organization that has embraced digital transformation and transformed its industry. Zara is a fashion retailer that has disrupted the industry by adopting a customer-centric approach to design, production, and distribution. Zara's approach to digital transformation includes using big data to analyze customer preferences, adopting agile methodologies to speed up production cycles, and using technology to optimize inventory management. Zara's approach has enabled it to respond quickly to changing customer preferences, reduce lead times, and increase customer satisfaction.

4. "We don't have adequate resources to support the Lean Digital transformation."

They may fail to invest in the necessary training and development programs that are required for the employees to gain new skills and adopt new ways of working. Without proper training, employees may find it difficult to adapt to the new digital systems and technologies, leading to a lack of adoption and failure of the transformation initiative.

5. "We lack alignment between different departments or teams within the organization."

It is crucial to have a shared vision and common goals across the organization to drive the Lean Digital transformation. Leaders must ensure that different teams are working collaboratively towards the common objectives of the transformation initiative. They should foster an environment that promotes open communication and collaboration among the teams to break down any silos that may hinder the transformation process.

6. "We can't do it because of certain external factors."

Many leaders give external reasons such as economic conditions or industry disruptions for the failure of Lean Digital transformation. While external factors may pose challenges, it is important to recognize that digital transformation is a long-term process that requires continuous effort and investment. Leaders must take a proactive approach to address these challenges by being agile and adaptable to changes in the business environment.

7. "We don't get support from board or senior management."

It is the responsibility of the leaders to convince and educate the senior management and board members about the benefits and importance of the transformation initiative. Leaders should be able to articulate a clear vision and business case for the initiative and demonstrate its potential for driving growth and innovation.

Key Takeaways

Leaders need to create a culture of continuous improvement within their organization, where employees are encouraged to identify and address inefficiencies and opportunities for improvement, thereby overcoming the common excuses that can derail lean and digital transformation initiatives.

3.4 Real Challenges to develop Lean culture and Digital Capability

While the benefits of lean and digital transformation are many, there are also several challenges that organizations face in developing a lean culture and digital capability. These challenges can be in the form of obstacles that must be promptly identified and overcome.

In this section, we will explore some of the real challenges that organizations face when developing these capabilities, and how they can arise due to a variety of reasons, such as resistance to change, lack of skills and knowledge, insufficient investment, and poor communication.

Here are some of the real challenges that organizations face in developing a lean culture and digital capability:

1. Resistance to Change: Resistance to change is a common challenge that organizations face when implementing lean and digital transformation initiatives. People are naturally resistant to change, especially if it means changing the way they work or the tools they use. Resistance to change can be due to several reasons, such as fear of the unknown, lack of understanding of the benefits of change, and perceived loss of control. To overcome this challenge, organizations need to communicate the benefits of the transformation and involve employees in the change process.

2. Lack of Skills and Knowledge: Developing a lean culture and digital capability requires employees to have the necessary skills and knowledge. However, many organizations struggle with a lack of skilled employees. This is particularly true for digital transformation, where there is a shortage of skilled professionals. To address this challenge, organizations need to invest in training and development programs to upskill their employees.

3. Insufficient Investment: Implementing a lean culture and digital capability requires investment in technology, tools, and infrastructure. However, many organizations struggle with insufficient investment, which can limit the effectiveness of their transformation initiatives. To address this challenge, organizations need to make a long-term investment in their transformation initiatives and ensure that they have the necessary resources to achieve their goals.

4. Poor Communication: Communication is essential to the success of any transformation initiative. However, many organizations struggle with poor communication, which can lead to misunderstandings and resistance to change. To overcome this challenge, organizations need to communicate clearly and regularly with their employees, customers, and other stakeholders. They should also involve employees in the decision-making process and encourage feedback and suggestions.

5. Lack of Leadership Support: Developing a lean culture and digital capability requires strong leadership support. However, many organizations struggle with a lack of leadership support, which can hinder the success of their transformation initiatives. To address this challenge, organizations need to ensure that their leaders are fully committed to the transformation and are actively involved in its implementation.

6. Difficulty in Measuring ROI: Measuring the return on investment (ROI) of lean and digital transformation initiatives can be challenging. This is particularly true for digital transformation, where the benefits are often intangible and difficult to quantify. To address this challenge, organizations need to define clear metrics and KPIs to measure the effectiveness of their transformation initiatives.

7. Lack of Alignment with Business Strategy: Developing a lean culture and digital capability should be aligned with the organization's overall business strategy. However, many organizations struggle with a lack of alignment, which can lead to a disjointed approach to transformation. To address this challenge, organizations need to ensure that their transformation initiatives are aligned with their overall business strategy and goals.

8. Resistance from Stakeholders: Resistance from stakeholders, such as customers, partners, and suppliers, can also be a challenge for organizations implementing lean and digital transformation initiatives. These stakeholders may have their own way of doing things and may be resistant to change. To address this challenge, organizations need to involve their stakeholders in the transformation process and communicate the benefits of the transformation to them.

Key Takeaways

Apparently, developing lean culture and digital capability is a complex and challenging process that requires a multifaceted approach built on a shift in mindset and behaviour. As such, organizations need to be prepared to invest in the necessary resources, communicate effectively, and align their transformation initiatives with their overall business strategy.

3.5 Lean Digital Maturity in Different Sectors

Lean Digital transformation is a journey that organizations need to embark on to remain competitive and relevant in the fast-changing digital world. Every sector faces unique challenges and opportunities in implementing Lean Digital transformation. We will explore the maturity of Lean Digital transformation in different sectors in this part of the section.

1. Manufacturing Sector: The manufacturing sector has been an early adopter of Lean principles, and the use of digital technologies is becoming increasingly common. The integration of Lean and digital technologies has enabled manufacturers to reduce waste, improve quality, and increase efficiency. For example, General Electric (GE) has successfully implemented a Lean Digital transformation, resulting in increased productivity and reduced costs. For example, sensors can be used to monitor equipment performance in real-time, allowing for predictive maintenance and reducing downtime. GE used sensors and data analytics to optimize its manufacturing processes, resulting in a 20% reduction in cycle time and a 50% increase in productivity. Also, with the advent of Industry 4.0 technologies, manufacturers are increasingly integrating digital technologies into their processes, creating a new paradigm of digital manufacturing. With the use of automation, machine learning, and predictive maintenance, manufacturers can optimize their production processes, reduce costs, and improve quality. Worthy of mention also, is the Internet of Things (IoT), created to improve productivity and increase overall efficiency.

2. Healthcare Sector: The healthcare sector has traditionally been slow to adopt digital technologies due to concerns around data privacy and regulatory constraints. However, this sector is ripe for Lean Digital transformation. The integration of digital technologies has the potential to improve patient outcomes, reduce costs, and increase efficiency. The use of electronic health records (EHRs) and telemedicine has already made significant improvements in healthcare delivery. For example, the Cleveland Clinic, a leading healthcare provider, has implemented a Lean Digital transformation resulting in reduced patient wait times, improved patient outcomes, and increased efficiency. Similarly, telemedicine and remote monitoring have made it possible for patients to receive medical care without physically visiting a doctor's office or hospital, reducing the risk of infection and increasing convenience.

3. Financial Sector: The financial sector is increasingly using digital technologies to improve customer experience, reduce costs, and increase efficiency. The use of Lean principles has helped financial institutions to streamline their processes and reduce waste. Banks are increasingly using data analytics and machine learning to improve and personalize customer experience, reduce fraud, and optimize their operations. For example, Capital One, a leading financial institution, has implemented a Lean Digital transformation resulting in increased efficiency and reduced costs (source).

4. Retail Sector: The retail sector is using digital technologies to improve customer experience, reduce costs, and increase efficiency. The integration of Lean principles has enabled retailers to streamline their processes and reduce waste. The sector has undergone a significant digital transformation in recent years, with e-commerce giants like Amazon driving a shift towards online shopping. Also, Walmart, a leading retailer, has implemented a Lean Digital transformation resulting in increased efficiency and reduced costs. Walmart used data analytics to optimize its supply chain, resulting in a 15% reduction in inventory and a 17% reduction in transportation costs.

5. Education Sector: The education sector is increasingly using digital technologies to improve student outcomes, reduce costs, and increase efficiency. The use of Learning Management Systems (LMS) and online education platforms has already made significant improvements in education delivery. For example, Arizona State University has implemented a Lean Digital transformation resulting in improved student outcomes and increased efficiency. Arizona State University used data analytics to optimize its course offerings, resulting in a 90% retention rate and a 17% increase in graduation rates.

6. Transportation Sector: The transportation industry is another sector where Lean Digital Transformation can have a significant impact. By integrating digital technologies such as GPS tracking, predictive analytics, and autonomous vehicles, transportation companies can optimize routes, reduce fuel consumption, and enhance safety.

7. Government Sector: The government sector is using digital technologies to improve citizen services, reduce costs, and increase efficiency. The use of Lean principles has helped governments to streamline their processes and reduce waste. For example, the city of Boston has implemented a Lean Digital transformation resulting in improved citizen services and increased efficiency. The city of Boston used data analytics to optimize its transportation system, resulting in a 10% reduction in commute times and a 5% reduction in transportation costs (source).

8. Information technology (IT) industry: The IT industry has been at the head of the Lean Digital Transformation, especially since Agile methods have become so popular. Early adopters like Microsoft and IBM opened the way for a change in how software is made, with a focus on iterative processes and working together with customers.

As Lean ideas got better, businesses like Google started to use a more comprehensive method. Google uses Lean concepts in more areas than just making software. For example, they use them in project management, allocating resources, and interacting with customers. Google's company culture is built around the idea of constant improvement and cutting down on waste. Google's methods for making software, managing projects, and putting the customer first show that it is committed to Lean Digital Transformation. The fact that the company did well shows that Lean concepts work in the IT field.

9. The fast-moving consumer goods (FMCG) industry: The FMCG industry, which used to be based on physical supply chains and old-fashioned retail, has changed a lot. The consumer goods giant Procter & Gamble (P&G) shows how the industry has changed to react to digital realities. P&G knew that it needed to use Lean concepts to handle the complexity of its supply chain. As part of its Lean journey, P&G uses data analytics to predict demand, improve inventory management, and keep track of its supply chain. By making choices based on data, P&G cuts down on waste, makes sure there are enough products in stock to meet customer demand, and minimises inventory levels. Procter & Gamble (P&G) P&G's use of Lean concepts in its operations and supply chain shows how a traditional industry can use digital transformation to become more efficient and improve customer satisfaction.

10. E-commerce: Because e-commerce is so active, it was one of the first industries to use Lean methods. Amazon was one of the first companies to use Lean methods, and they are now built into the way they run their business. Jeff Bezos's idea of "two-pizza teams" is similar to a Lean way of organising teams, which encourages flexibility and effective working together. Amazon's advanced use of AI and ML for supply chain optimisation, inventory management, and personalised customer experiences is a good example of advanced Lean integration in the sector. A big part of the company's Lean Digital Transformation is its dedication to always getting better and putting the customer first. Amazon's Lean journey shows how Lean Digital Transformation can be used on a large scale and in the fast-paced E-commerce industry. The company's unwavering focus on new ideas and efficiency has changed the rules for the business.

Key Takeaways

In brevity, Lean Digital transformation is essential for organizations to remain competitive and relevant in today's fast-changing digital world. Every sector faces unique challenges and opportunities in implementing Lean Digital transformation, and the maturity level of implementation varies across different sectors. However, the integration of Lean principles and digital technologies has already proven to be successful in improving efficiency, reducing waste, and increasing productivity in various sectors.

3.6 World needs Transformational Leaders not just Followers

There once was a business named InnovateTech that was at the forefront of digital transformation in a world rife with difficulties and possibilities. Emma Williams, the CEO, was a firm believer in the ability of transformational leadership to effect lasting change within and beyond the company.

To emphasise the need for transformational leaders, Emma called a meeting of her executive staff. She kicked off the discussion by describing her goals.

The environment we live in today requires transformational leaders," Emma told her team. To successfully traverse the challenges of the digital transition, we need people who can motivate and equip others to do the same. We can't just follow along; we have to be the ones who initiate change.

Alex, the chief innovator, shared his thoughts. Emma, define a transformative leader and tell me why we need them.

Emma cracked a grin and used an example from her own life to make her point. "Picture a ship's captain navigating perilous seas. A transactional leader would prioritise current initiatives to keep the ship afloat. A transformational leader, on the other hand, would chart a new course, unite the crew, and motivate them to accept and even embrace change in order to expand their organisation's horizons.

She elaborated, "Transformational leaders push the boundaries of what is possible. They push their teams to think beyond the box and give them the freedom to pursue novel opportunities. They foster a common purpose and an attitude of constant progress.

Emma stressed that CEOs are not the only place to find transformative leaders. They can appear anywhere in an organisation, from entry-level workers to upper management. Their impact is not limited to the group they directly manage but rather permeates the entire company.

Researchers and subject-matter experts were consulted in order to have a deeper comprehension of transformative leadership and its effects. They looked into the writings of well-known authorities on leadership, such as Bernard Bass and James MacGregor Burns, who have done substantial work defining and studying transformational leadership.

They also looked to real-world examples of transformative leaders for guidance, such as Elon Musk, whose innovative approach has disrupted several industries, and Indra Nooyi, whose leadership converted PepsiCo into a sustainable and purpose-driven business.

The group came to see the tremendous potential in transformational leadership when they applied it to their own digital transformation. They promised to improve their leadership abilities, create a more trustworthy environment, and give their staff more agency in driving change.

Incredible growth was seen at InnovateTech throughout the years. The company gained a reputation for its forward-thinking strategies, supportive office culture, and speedy response to changing market conditions. Throughout the company, transformational leaders emerged and fueled a culture of constant change. InnovateTech's teamwork typified the potential for transformational leadership to influence the future for the better.

As the world rapidly advances towards digital transformation, organizations need leaders at their core who can inspire and drive change. Transformational leadership is a leadership style that emphasizes inspiring and motivating employees to innovate and create change that leads to the growth and success of the organization. In contrast to transactional leaders who focus on rewarding good performance and punishing poor performance, transformational leaders focus on creating a culture of innovation and collaboration.

In the context of Lean Digital transformation, transformational leadership is crucial for success. Transformational leaders can help organizations overcome the challenges of developing a lean culture and digital capability, as discussed in previous sections. In this section, we will discuss the characteristics of transformational leaders and why they are essential for Lean Digital transformation.

3.6.1 Characteristics of Transformational Leaders

1. Visionary: Transformational leaders must have a clear vision and purpose for their organizations. They must be able to see the big picture and articulate a compelling vision for the future. They must be able to communicate this vision to their teams in a way that motivates them to work towards a common goal. By creating a shared sense of purpose and direction, and empower their teams to take ownership of their work and contribute to the overall success of the organization, they will be able to inspire their teams to work towards this vision, even in the face of adversity or setbacks.'

2. Inspirational: Transformational leaders inspire and motivate their employees to be the best they can be. They encourage creativity and innovation, foster a positive culture, and empower their employees to take ownership of their work. They lead by example and demonstrate a strong work ethic, integrity, and respect for their employees.

3. Empathetic: Transformational leaders are able to connect with their teams on a personal level and understand their needs and concerns. They are able to create a culture of trust and respect, where everyone feels valued and heard.

In essence, transformational leaders must build strong relationships with their teams, which will engender mutual trust and self-esteem. They must also be able to show empathy and understanding towards their teams, and create a culture that supports mental health and well-being.

4. Strategic Thinkers: Transformational leaders are strategic thinkers who have a long-term perspective on their organization's goals. They are not reactive but rather proactive in identifying opportunities for growth and improvement. They prioritize tasks and delegate responsibilities to their team members according to their strengths and abilities.

5. Collaborative: Transformational leaders recognize the value of collaboration and teamwork. They foster an environment where employees feel comfortable sharing their ideas and opinions, and they encourage open communication. They build relationships based on trust and respect and empower their employees to work together to achieve their goals.

6. Decisive: Transformational leaders are able to make tough decisions and take decisive action, even in the face of uncertainty or risk. They are able to weigh the pros and cons of different options and make informed decisions that are in the best interest of the organization.

7. Accountable: Transformational leaders take responsibility for their actions and are accountable for the outcomes of their decisions. They are able to learn from their mistakes and use them as opportunities for growth and improvement.

3.6.2 Why Transformational Leaders are Essential for Lean Digital Transformation?

1. They Drive Change

Transformational leaders are change agents who are not satisfied with the status quo. They inspire and motivate their employees to embrace change and create new and innovative ways of working. They challenge the traditional way of doing things and seek out new opportunities for growth and improvement.

2. They Build a Culture of Innovation

Transformational leaders foster a culture of innovation and creativity. They encourage their employees to take risks and experiment with new ideas. They provide their teams with the necessary resources and support to turn their ideas into reality. This type of culture is essential for organizations undergoing digital transformation.

3. They Inspire their Employees

Transformational leaders inspire their employees to be the best they can be. They create a positive work environment where employees feel valued and empowered. They provide their employees wit

h opportunities for growth and development, which helps to retain top talent.

4. They are Strategic Thinkers

Transformational leaders have a long-term perspective on their organization's goals. They are strategic thinkers who identify opportunities for growth and improvement. They prioritize tasks and delegate responsibilities to their team members according to their strengths and abilities.

5. They Prioritize Collaboration and Teamwork

Transformational leaders recognize the value of collaboration and teamwork. They foster an environment where employees feel comfortable sharing their ideas and opinions, and they encourage open communication. They build relationships based on trust and respect and empower their employees to work together to achieve their goals.

6. They have the Ability to Communicate Effectively

They are adept at conveying their vision to their followers and inspiring them to work towards it. They are also able to listen actively and take feedback from their team, which helps in building a strong bond and trust between them. This kind of trust is essential for creating an environment of innovation and creativity, where individuals feel comfortable sharing their ideas and opinions.

7. They have Staunch Emotional Intelligence

They understand the impact of their actions on their followers and strive to build positive relationships with them. They are also able to manage their own emotions effectively, especially in high-pressure situations, which helps them maintain focus and clarity of thought.

8. Transformational Leaders also tend to be Ethical in their Approach

They are committed to doing the right thing, even if it means making tough decisions that may not be popular. They are transparent in their dealings and hold themselves and their team accountable for their actions.

Overall, the world needs more transformational leaders who can guide us through the complex challenges of the 21st century. These leaders will be able to drive innovation, inspire collaboration, and create a better future for all. As Mahatma Gandhi said, "Be the change you wish to see in the world." By becoming transformational leaders ourselves, we can inspire others to do the same and create a ripple effect that will transform the world.

Key Takeaways

Aspirational and motivating vision and mission are characteristics of transformational leaders. They motivate people by seeing a brighter future and working hard to make it a reality. High levels of emotional intelligence are a feature of transformational leaders, allowing them to empathise with and meet the needs of their teams. Trust, empathy, and respect are the cornerstones of their relationships.

To sum up, the world needs leaders who can transform their followers and the world around them. These pioneers can see the future clearly, have strong interpersonal skills, encourage teamwork, and welcome change.

Chapter Summary

- Lean Digital is not just a buzzword or a lipstick, but a key enabler for businesses to transform and succeed in today's digital age, if approached strategically. By embracing digital technologies and adopting a Lean Digital approach, companies can streamline their processes, eliminate waste, and create a culture of continuous improvement.

- However, this requires a cultural shift that starts with strong leadership, effective communication, and a commitment to building a culture of continuous improvement.

- Also, developing lean culture and digital capability is a complex and challenging process that requires a multifaceted approach. Organizations need to address the challenges of changing mindsets and behavior, keeping up with rapidly evolving technology, integrating technology into existing processes, addressing resistance to change, and honing analytic capabilities.

- By embracing Lean Digital principles and developing transformational leaders who will overcome the common excuses that can derail lean and digital initiatives, organizations can build digital capabilities, create new opportunities, and drive growth in a rapidly changing world to deliver significant benefits for their organizations.

- As Henry Ford famously said, "If you always do what you've always done, you'll always get what you've always got." It's time to embrace change and lead the way towards a brighter future.

Key Questions for Readers

- What role does Lean Digital play in facilitating digital transformation? What are any concrete case studies or illustrations of its usefulness?

- What are some unexpected causes of lean and digital projects' failure? If businesses want a better likelihood of success, how can they do something about these issues?

- When it comes to implementing lean and digital transformation, what are the most frequent justifications that top-level management gives? How can we get through these justifications and create an environment where digital innovation and adoption thrive?

- How difficult is it for businesses to implement a lean culture and build digital capabilities? How can we overcome these obstacles to lay the groundwork for a smooth transition?

- How does the level of Lean Digital maturity differ between industries? What causes certain sectors to be more or less developed than others, and why?

- The necessity for transformational leaders, as opposed to mere followers, is why. How can people learn to develop the traits that make a leader truly transformative?

Part Four

Focus Three: It's a people Game

Why is it everyone's responsibility?

"Continuous improvement is better than delayed perfection."

~Mark Twain

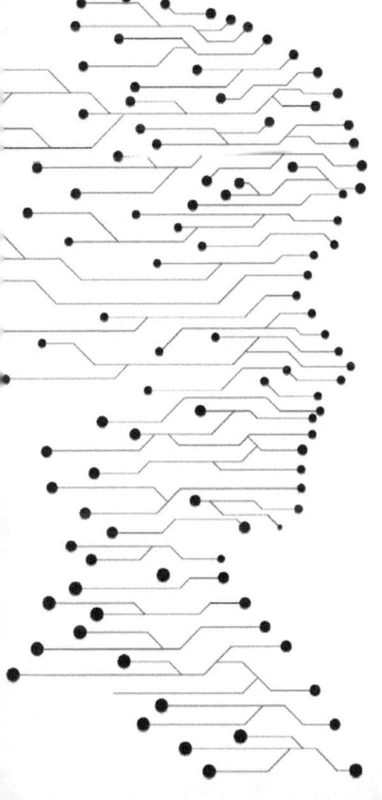

"Lean and digital are two potent approaches that may drive substantial change in organisations." However, they work best together and are less effective when used individually. Digital technology offers automation, data-driven decision-making, and improved customer experiences; lean concepts help eliminate waste and improve productivity. The impact on firms can be revolutionary when lean and digital are combined. This chapter delves into the reasons why these methods are incompatible with one another and how they might be combined for long-term success.

Team, department, and function Silos are the boundaries that prevent communication and cooperation inside an organisation. Separate implementations of lean and digital efforts tend to cause these divisions, leading to lost opportunities, inefficiencies, and poor outcomes. Let's look at ten cases to see how operating in silos can backfire:

- Delays, repeated work, and misalignment can occur when teams have issues communicating critical information across departments due to a lack of lean practises and digital technology integration.

- Non-value-added procedures in processes are not being identified or removed because of silos, which prevent cross-functional collaboration. While digital technology can automate and streamline many procedures, inefficiency will remain without a lean mentality.

- When information is kept in isolated silos across several teams, it becomes difficult to see the big picture. This hinders the realisation of data-driven insights that might drive continual improvement and hinders the making of effective choices.

- Whereas digital transformations frequently attempt to improve customer service, lean initiatives typically aim to reduce waste. Independent pursuit of these goals can lead to conflicting objectives that slow you down and prevent you from reaching your full potential.

- Isolated departments are more likely to be resistant to embracing new technology and practises since they are focused on meeting their own objectives. This obstruction hinders the progress of the change as a whole.

- A customer's experience can become fragmented when they have to deal with different departments inside a firm, such as sales, marketing, and customer support. Customer satisfaction and loyalty can be negatively impacted when these departments work in silos.

- Innovation flourishes in environments that foster teamwork and the exchange of different types of perspectives. The organisation's adaptability and success are hampered when lean and digital projects are implemented in silos.

- Duplicated work and wasted resources might occur when various departments aren't integrated with one another. This can happen if the goals of your lean initiatives and your digital projects aren't aligned, resulting in wasted time and money.

- Insufficient visibility into the status and results of efforts may result from the existence of silos. Because of this, the company's capacity to make data-driven decisions is impaired, and it becomes more challenging to assess the results of lean or digital initiatives.

- Opportunity is lost because of a lack of communication and the inability to share knowledge effectively between departments. Organisations risk missing out on connections and failing to realise digital and lean's full revolutionary potential if they are implemented in silos.

In conclusion, it is clear that lean and digital cannot function independently. To realise their full potential and secure long-term success, businesses must integrate these methods. Organisations may develop a culture that supports Lean principles, innovation, and improved customer experiences by removing barriers to communication and cooperation and instituting a culture of collaboration based on those principles.

4.1.1 Harmful Effects of Separated Departments and Workforces

There was once a prosperous city that was home to a manufacturing firm known as Precision Engineering. It was proud of the quality products it produced using lean methods. There was a lean team within the organisation that was committed to streamlining operations and eliminating waste. However, despite their best efforts, the outcomes were not particularly impressive.

A digital startup company called TechSolutions was located in another part of town. To improve their customers' digital experiences, they used advanced technologies and data analytics. They were well known for their quickness to respond to shifting customer preferences.

The CEOs of Precision Engineering and TechSolutions crossed paths at a regional business conference one day. They began talking after becoming fascinated by one another's fields of study. Precision Engineering's CEO, Tom, vented his dissatisfaction about the lack of results from lean programmes. Sarah, CEO of TechSolutions, understood his plight because she had experienced similar difficulties with digital transformations leading to long-term success. As they talked further, they saw that they were both struggling with the same problem: they were working in isolation. The factory floor was the sole domain of lean initiatives, while the consumer interface was the primary target of digital reforms.

It became clear that combining lean and digital was the key to realising their full potential.

Tom and Sarah's insight was a catalyst for their endeavour to combine lean and digital in precision engineering. Lean specialists, data scientists, software engineers, and CX experts all came together to form this interdisciplinary group. They banded together to eliminate barriers and develop a streamlined process for using lean thinking and digital tools.

The results were amazing. Here are a few of the most significant shifts they saw:

- The multidisciplinary group was able to analyse departmental processes and find the underlying causes of waste and inefficiency. They could make better, more timely decisions with the help of digital tools that allowed them to see data in real time.

- The team was able to pinpoint bottlenecks and implement systemic improvements in procedures due to the combination of lean and digital. By digitising routine processes, they cut down on unnecessary errors made by humans and freed up manpower.

- By removing barriers, the group was able to obtain information from all departments. They utilised advanced analytics to discover previously unseen trends and patterns, paving the way for proactive measures and ongoing progress.

- Precision Engineering has improved their customer service by working together with their lean and digital teams to design unique experiences for each client. They used digital platforms to learn from customers, respond rapidly to shifting tastes, and offer streamlined services from ordering through delivery.

- The culture of experimentation and invention was encouraged by the combination of lean and digital, leading to the development of agile innovation. Employees from all divisions were encouraged to share their perspectives, which led to innovative responses to old problems

Precision Engineering and TechSolutions' experience shows that lean and digital processes may flourish when combined rather than operating independently. An environment where lean concepts and digital technology reinforce each other can be created when businesses align their aims, remove barriers, and encourage collaboration.

Implementing Lean Digital in isolated departments is ineffective. It calls for a team effort that cuts over traditional organisational structures to encourage cooperation and open lines of communication among all involved.

Inefficiencies, knowledge gaps, and decreased collaboration can all result from having several teams and departments work on Lean Digital at the same time. As a result, the organisation is hampered in its efforts to attain its full potential.

Ten real-world cases demonstrating the negative consequences of siloed departments and workforces serve as lessons, emphasising the need to eliminate these barriers and encourage cooperation in order to realise the full potential of Lean Digital.

Breaking down silos, encouraging openness, and building a culture of cooperation and communication across all departments and teams are essential for organisations to reap the full benefits of Lean Digital. With this connection, information can be shared, aims can be synchronised, and everyone can work together to bring about the desired digital change.

4.2 What Capabilities do Lean Digital Leaders should have?

Successful Lean Digital transformations are driven by strong leadership. To successfully exploit the relationship between lean concepts and digital technology, leaders need a special skill set only possessed by those who have mastered the art of leading via digital transformation. In this chapter, we discuss the skills and talents necessary for Lean Digital leaders to create lasting change in their organisations.

Precision Engineering was a factory in a thriving metropolis. The organisation had struggled to modernise for the digital age and make considerable progress through lean practises. The company's CEO, Tom, saw the need for a new sort of leader who could unite the company's traditional Lean values with the latest digital innovations. He embarked on a search for the ideal person to fill the role of Lean Digital Leader at the company.

Tom found Laura, a vibrant expert with extensive experience in lean techniques and digital transformation, after an exhaustive search. Laura had extensive experience leading lean programmes and a keen knowledge of the potential of digital technology, both of which had served her well in prior organisations. Tom promoted Laura to the position of Lean Digital Leader in Precision Engineering because of her impressive skills and forward thinking.

When Laura was hired, a fresh phase of growth and innovation began at the organisation. She was able to successfully steer the Lean Digital Transformation because of her exceptional skill set. Let's take a look at the skills that all great Lean Digital leaders need to have:

- Leaders in the Lean Digital space see clearly into the future and are able to convey that vision in a way that motivates and unites their teams. They promote a mindset of constant improvement and new ideas by emphasising the benefits of lean and digital integration.

- These leaders are strategic thinkers who see the bigger picture of what lean and digital changes could mean for their organisations. They make sure the transformation initiatives are meaningful and effective by coordinating the lean and digital strategies with the overall business goals.

- The ability to manage resistance to change and triumph over challenges encountered along the transformation process is a hallmark of Lean Digital leaders. To promote change acceptance and maintenance, they effectively communicate, form alliances, and provide an atmosphere of urgency.

- These leaders facilitate collaboration across departments and functions to eliminate silos and promote information sharing. They get that interdisciplinary groups are key to making lasting progress on multiple fronts at once.

- Knowledge of digital technology, trends, and their prospective uses is a hallmark of Lean Digital leaders. They monitor the technological landscape, make use of data-driven insights, and propel digital innovation throughout the company.

- These leaders have expertise in the Lean philosophy as well as its associated tools and practises. They direct groups towards a culture of continual improvement by helping them recognise and get rid of waste.

- Decisions are driven by data analytics, which is used by Lean Digital leaders. Their knowledge of data collection, analysis, and interpretation allows them to spot areas for development and propel evidence-based decisions.

- These leaders approach Lean Digital transformation with a focus on the customer's value and experience. They encourage a client-focused mindset that helps lean and digital projects succeed in making clients happier and more loyal.

- Strong emotional intelligence allows Lean Digital leaders to empathise with, motivate, and inspire their people. They recognise the emotional toll that change can take on people and work to foster a setting where workers feel valued and respected.

- These leaders are committed to their own growth and possess a growth mindset, which allows them to learn and adapt on the job. They are always on the lookout for new ways to expand their knowledge of lean practises and cutting-edge IT tools.

- Lean Digital leaders embody these skills to propel transformational results and position their organisations for success in the digital age. They are essential in establishing norms that encourage experimentation, creativity, and flexibility.

Key Takeaways

Leaders in the field of Lean Digital should be well-versed in both Lean principles and digital technologies. They should be the ones to unite the two sides of the business and get everyone on the same page.

Leaders in Lean Digital should be able to inspire and motivate their teams, push for meaningful change, and cultivate an environment that encourages constant development and new ideas.

Lean Digital leaders must have the skills to effectively communicate, collaborate, and deal with complexity. Leaders in the digital transformation space need to be able to articulate the vision, gather support from key participants, exploit the benefits, and overcome the threats that come with the transition.

4.3 Do People Really Understand the Meaning of Agility?

"In today's rapidly changing business environment, agility has become a buzzword frequently used to characterise organisations that can quickly adapt and thrive despite change. However, do individuals comprehend the basic concept and significance of agility? This chapter explores the real significance of agility as it pertains to Lean Digital Transformation. We investigate its basic principles and the manner in which agile businesses leverage the proper Lean Digital capabilities to drive transformational change."

Imagine you are an employee at Precision Manufacturing, a traditional manufacturing corporation. For many years, the company adhered to a strict hierarchical structure in which decisions were made at the top and trickled down through management levels. Change was gradual, and there was widespread opposition to novel ideas and methods. Innovation seemed like a distant fantasy.

The CEO once gathered the entire organisation for a crucial announcement. Precision Manufacturing will undergo Lean Digital Transformation to become an agile organisation, he declared. The room was filled with enthusiasm and intrigue. But amid the excitement, there was also a sense of unease. What did agility actually entail? How would it affect their duties and the entire organisation?

In the context of Lean Digital Transformation, agility is not limited to the ability to respond rapidly to market changes. It surpasses quickness and precision. True agility requires cultivating an attitude of continuous refinement, adaptability, and collaboration. It necessitates that organisations adopt Lean principles and utilise digital technologies to drive transformational change.

Let's examine five agile organisations that have effectively transformed themselves by adopting the appropriate Lean Digital capabilities:

Spotify: As the industry leader in music streaming, Spotify has embraced adaptability to remain ahead of the curve. They have established cross-functional teams referred to as "squads" that are responsible for particular product areas. These squads operate independently, utilising Lean principles and digital tools to perpetually enhance their products and adapt to shifting customer preferences.

Amazon: Amazon is well-known for its customer-centric focus and swift innovation. They have established a culture of experimentation and continuous refinement as a result of their Lean Digital Transformation. Utilising data analytics and digital technologies, they collect real-time customer feedback, adapt their offerings, and enhance operational efficiency.

Airbnb: Airbnb disrupted the hospitality industry through the use of digital technologies and an agile mindset. They perpetually iterate and enhance their platform, enabling seamless connections between hosts and guests. Their Lean Digital capabilities enable them to adapt their business model, rapidly scale, and respond to market demands.

Zappos: The corporate culture at Zappos, an online shoe and clothing retailer, embraces agility. They emphasise employee empowerment and cultivate a sense of ownership and independence. Their Lean Digital capabilities allow them to respond rapidly to customer requirements, test new concepts, and continuously enhance the customer experience.

Tesla: Tesla's success stems from the company's ability to integrate Lean principles with digital innovation. Utilising data-driven insights and cutting-edge technologies, they perpetually iterate and improve their electric vehicles. Their Lean Digital capabilities allow them to foster innovation, optimise their manufacturing processes, and produce high-quality goods.

These agile companies demonstrate that agility is not an abstract concept but rather a concrete reality attained by effectively combining Lean principles and digital capabilities. Fostering continuous development, adaptability, and collaboration requires a shift in perspective, organisational structure, and culture.

Key Takeaways

It's possible that everyone has a misunderstanding of what agility really means. Agility is the capacity to quickly adjust to new conditions, whether in the realm of business, technology, or one's own life.

Agility is more than just the capacity to shift direction quickly or adapt to new circumstances; it also involves welcoming and even seeking out novelty and new chances.

Individuals and businesses alike would do well to educate themselves on the topic of agility and its significance in today's fast-paced and uncertain world. Because of this insight, they are able to use agility to their advantage whenever a new obstacle or opportunity presents itself.

4.4 Why do we need Transformational Leaders to make it happen?

Leadership is the engine that powers effective Lean Digital Transformations. An organisation's ability to adapt to new circumstances depends on the leadership team's ability to motivate, direct, and empower employees during the transition. The importance of transformational leaders in achieving Lean Digital Transformation is discussed in this chapter. We also look at ten case studies of transformational leaders who guided their organisations through successful change." Imagine a world where businesses never evolve because they have become rigid in their ways. Such an environment restricts development, and businesses have a hard time adjusting to the ever-changing demands of the market. Leaders who can spark transformation and lead their companies into a better future are especially valuable in such an environment.

You may be asking yourself, "Why do we need transformational leaders in order to implement Lean Digital Transformation?" The key is in their capacity to encourage a shared vision, motivate others, and propel substantial progress.

There are a few distinguishing characteristics shared by all transformational leaders:

- A clear vision of the organisation's future is essential for a transformational leader. They share this goal with their groups to give them focus and motivation.These leaders motivate and inspire their employees to accept change and continuously improve. They inspire eagerness and enthusiasm for the process of change that lies ahead.

- Responsible delegation and the encouragement of individual initiative are hallmarks of the transformational leadership style. They help people reach their full potential by providing them with the means to do so.

- As a form of intellectual stimulation, these leaders promote an environment where people are comfortable questioning established norms and trying new things. They encourage their employees to think critically and creatively by providing them with intellectual stimulation.

- Transformational leaders provide a good example by leading by doing. They model the attitudes and actions they want to see in their teams, gaining the respect and admiration of their peers.

Let's look at transformative leaders who led their companies via digital learning with great success.

- **Microsoft CEO Satya Nadella:** Under Nadella's leadership, Microsoft shifted its strategy to prioritise the cloud and mobile devices over software. Microsoft's successful transition to the digital age was led by his foresight and leadership.

- **Tim Cook (Apple):** Tim Cook succeeded Steve Jobs as Apple's chief executive officer, and he has overseen the company's rapid expansion and innovative new products. His foresight and drive to improve operations spurred Apple's digital transition.

- **Mary Barra (General Motors):** Mary Barra reshaped General Motors by placing an emphasis on creativity, welcoming cutting-edge technologies, and emphasising the needs of consumers. Under her direction, the company's standing in the car industry has been restored.

- **Sundar Pichai (Google):** Sundar Pichai has been instrumental in guiding Google's evolution into a diversified tech giant. Google's rapid development and expansion can be directly attributed to his emphasis on AI and data-driven decision-making.

- **Ginni Rometty (IBM):** Ginni Rometty led IBM's transformation by reorienting the firm to new technologies, including artificial intelligence (AI), cloud computing (CC), and blockchain. Under her direction, IBM was able to adapt to the ever-changing conditions of the digital world.

- **Mary Dillon (Ulta Beauty):** Mary Dillon completely revamped Ulta Beauty by focusing on the client experience through the use of cutting-edge information and communication technologies. The company's expansion in the cosmetics retail sector may be directly attributed to her foresight and focus on customers

- **Brian Chesky (Airbnb):** Brian Chesky transformed Airbnb from a fledgling company into a global marketplace, thereby upending the whole hospitality business. His innovative approach to business and emphasis on customer satisfaction have altered the way people plan trips and reserve lodgings forever.

- **Alan Mulally (Ford Motor Company):** Instilling a culture of collaboration, transparency, and data-driven decision-making, Ford Motor Company was led through a successful Lean Digital Transformation under the leadership of Alan Mulally. His direction reshaped Ford's business and set it up for sustained growth.

- **Alibaba Group's Daniel Zhang:** He was instrumental in the company's rise to prominence as an online retailer around the world. Alibaba's rise and success can be directly attributed to his strategic foresight, concentration on digital innovation, and dedication to the company's customers.

- **Angela Ahrendts (formerly of Apple and Burberry):** Angela Ahrendts oversaw groundbreaking changes at both companies. To boost customer engagement and brand loyalty, she prioritised building seamless omnichannel experiences and utilising digital technology.

Leaders like these epitomise the important role they play in propelling successful Lean Digital Transformations. Their capacity to plan ahead, inspire people, and give them power has helped their businesses prosper in the digital age.

Key Takeaways

Leaders who can inspire and enable transformations are crucial to their success. They may build a sense of purpose and commitment in their teams by inspiring and motivating people, developing a compelling vision, and leading by example.

Leaders who are able to bring about transformation in an organisation are those who are capable of handling ambiguity, adapting to new situations, and convincing others of the necessity of change.

Successful transformational initiatives can be implemented because of the leadership of transformational leaders who have the qualities and skills to drive innovation, empower people, and create an atmosphere that promotes continual improvement and growth.

Transformative Leaders

Tim Cook succeeded Steve Jobs as Apple's chief executive officer, and he has overseen the company's rapid expansion and innovative new products. His foresight and drive to improve operations spurred Apple's digital transition.

Satya Nadella's leadership, Microsoft shifted its strategy to prioritise the cloud and mobile devices over software. Microsoft's successful transition to the digital age was led by his foresight and leadership.

Mary Barra (General Motors), Mary Barra reshaped General Motors by placing an emphasis on creativity, welcoming cutting-edge technologies, and emphasising the needs of consumers. Under her direction, the company's standing in the car industry has been restored.

Sundar Pichai (Google), Sundar Pichai has been instrumental in guiding Google's evolution into a diversified tech giant. Google's rapid development and expansion can be directly attributed to his emphasis on AI and data-driven decision-making.

Ginni Rometty (IBM), Ginni Rometty led IBM's transformation by reorienting the firm to new technologies, including artificial intelligence (AI), cloud computing (CC), and blockchain. Under her direction, IBM was able to adapt to the ever-changing conditions of the digital world.

Mary Dillon (Ulta Beauty), completely revamped Ulta Beauty by focusing on the client experience through the use of cutting-edge information and communication technologies. The company's expansion in the cosmetics retail sector may be directly attributed to her foresight and focus on customers

Brian Chesky (Airbnb), transformed Airbnb from a fledgling company into a global marketplace, thereby upending the whole hospitality business. His innovative approach to business and emphasis on customer satisfaction have altered the way people plan trips and reserve lodgings forever.

Alan Mulally (Ford Motor Company), Instilling a culture of collaboration, transparency, and data-driven decision-making, Ford Motor Company was led through a successful Lean Digital Transformation under the leadership of Alan Mulally. His direction reshaped Ford's business and set it up for sustained growth.

Alibaba Group's Daniel Zhang, He was instrumental in the company's rise to prominence as an online retailer around the world. Alibaba's rise and success can be directly attributed to his strategic foresight, concentration on digital innovation, and dedication to the company's customers.

Angela Ahrendts (formerly of Apple and Burberry)
Angela Ahrendts oversaw groundbreaking changes at both companies. To boost customer engagement and brand loyalty, she prioritised building seamless omnichannel experiences and utilising digital technology.

Figure 9: *Transformative Leaders*

Lean concepts and digital technologies have come together to produce a potent catalyst for organisational success in the field of Lean Digital Transformation. Transformative leaders, however, are the ones who have the ability to successfully handle the complex interplay between Lean, digital, and people. Focusing on the importance of Transformational Leadership 2.0, this chapter delves into the Lean Digital Transformation Model. To guarantee the success of Lean Digital Transformations, we look into the importance of people's support and the necessity of a balance between personal and professional lives.

Transformational Leadership 2.0

"Transformational Leadership 2.0" is a way of thinking about leadership that blends Lean ideas with digital technologies to make processes more efficient, improve customer value, and make businesses more efficient in the digital age. This method is based on Lean thinking, which started in manufacturing and became famous thanks to Toyota. Its main goals are to get rid of waste, encourage continuous improvement, and give customers what they want. Lean concepts help organisations get through the complicated process of digital transformation by encouraging flexibility, new ideas, and putting the customer first.

Transformational Leadership 2.0's Most Important Elements:

1. Agility:

Transformational Leadership 2.0 stresses flexibility, which lets businesses respond quickly to changes in the digital world. Iterative, collaborative, and customer-driven methods are possible with agile methodologies, which are often used in software development.

2. Focus on the customer:

Transformational Leadership 2.0 is all about putting the customer first. It focuses on businesses should always get feedback from customers, look at user data, and keep making small changes to their digital goods and services.

3. Getting rid of waste:

The main goal of lean concepts is to get rid of waste in time, resources, and processes. In the digital world, this means improving processes, getting rid of steps that aren't needed, and making sure that resources are used well.

4. Always getting better:

Continuous growth is one of the most important ideas in Transformational Leadership 2.0. Companies in the digital world are always trying to improve their methods, tools, and strategies by listening to customers, studying data, and watching how the market changes.

5. New ideas and trying new things:

Transformational Leadership 2.0 promotes an attitude of trying new things and coming up with new ideas. Teams are given the freedom to try out new ideas, fail, and learn from their mistakes. In a digital world that changes quickly, this method is necessary to stay competitive.

So If you are a Transformational Leader 2.0, then do equal use of technology driven by people.

Business Case Example

Example 1: Spotify's Agile Transformation

Spotify, a service for streaming music, did a Lean Digital Transformation by using Agile methods on a large scale. Their leadership team reorganised its development teams into "Squads," "Tribes," and "Guilds" to promote teamwork across departments, new ideas, and constant improvement. This change made it possible for Spotify to respond faster to user needs, keep its edge in the fast-paced digital music business, and release software updates more often.

Example 2:

As an ambitious CEO, Jake Thompson stood out for his technical expertise and ability to solve complex problems. At his company, a major manufacturer, he was tasked with directing a Lean Digital Transformation effort. Jake believed that, with his expertise in Lean concepts and cutting-edge digital tools, he could spearhead the transition and provide outstanding outcomes.

Jake's work-life balance, though, was a significant blind spot for him. He put his personal life on hold to focus on his career. The transformation project's long hours, relentless pressure, and heavy workload started taking their toll on his health.

Jake had a hard time getting other employees invested in the Lean Digital Transformation project at the outset. He was technically adept, but he overlooked the importance of people in leading successful Lean Digital Transformations. His team members were disengaged, underappreciated, and stressed out by the tempo of change.

As Jake learned more, he saw how the principles of Lean, digital technology, and people all worked together. The concept of Lean Digital transformation," he concluded, encompasses more than the simple adoption of new tools and the simplification of old ones. They focus on making individuals believe they have an opinion, encouraging a mindset of constant growth, and promoting an atmosphere of trust and teamwork.

When Jake realised how much his own personal and professional imbalance was hindering the change, that's when he finally awoke. His team's lack of enthusiasm and resistance reflected his own exhaustion and stress. It became clear that leaders with technical knowledge alone wouldn't be enough to ensure the success of Lean Digital Transformation; they also needed to be able to engage with their teams on a more personal level.

Jake set out on a journey for self-improvement. He understood the need to encourage a good work-life balance among his employees. He pushed for more candid exchanges, was there for his team members, and made sure their successes were rewarded. He made an effort to learn about and solve the problems and hopes of others on his team.

Jake's efforts to foster an atmosphere of openness and autonomy propelled the change forward. Staff morale was high, and as a result, productivity, initiative, and dedication all rose. Significant gains in productivity, client happiness, and financial health have already materialised thanks to the Lean Digital Transformation initiative.

Both the organisation and Jake's own life benefited greatly from Jake's commitment to transformative leadership. He understood that the success of the change was crucial to his happiness and satisfaction.

4.5.1 Lean, Digital, and People Relationships: Lean Digital can't Succeed in the Absence of Public Support

However, keep in mind that Lean Digital Transformations are about more than just new tech. Because people are the ones who actually adopt and push for these shifts, they are naturally at the heart of these transformations. Lean Digital Transformations are doomed to fail unless the people involved are fully committed and enthusiastic about the process.

Transformational Leadership 2.0 vs. Transformational Leadership: A Comparative Analysis

1. Principles:

Transformational Leadership 2.0 is based on Lean thought and stresses getting rid of waste, improving all the time, putting the customer first, and being flexible when using digital technologies and processes. Using Lean concepts in digital strategies and operations to improve workflows, cut down on waste, and give customers more value.

Whereas Transformational Leadership Focuses on inspiring and motivating followers, creating a shared goal, supporting personal growth, and encouraging intellectual curiosity among team members. It Focuses on leadership behaviours that bring about good change, transformation, and the growth of individuals within the organisation.

2. Focus and Scope:

Transformational Leadership 2.0 mainly on improving digital workflows, technologies, and processes to make them more efficient, cut down on waste, and make digital goods and services better. It Covers the whole digital value chain, from making software and running IT systems to caring for customers and analysing data.

Transformational Leadership focuses on the kinds of leadership actions that lead to good changes in the workplace, the growth of employees, and the creation of a shared goal for the future.It Covers how leaders work with different parts of an organisation, and how those actions affect the group's culture, communication, and general direction.

3. Strategies for Implementation:

Transformational Leadership 2.0 helps in bringing changes gradually using Agile methods, Lean concepts, and digital technologies. It encourages testing, development that happens in small steps, and feedback loops that never end.

Transformational Leaders show others how to do things, create a shared vision, question the status quo, and give others the power to act. Mostly about talking to each other, understanding, and making strong connections within the company.

4. How to Measure Success:

Transformational Leadership 2.0 uses Cycle time, lead time, customer satisfaction, and the efficiency of digital processes to measure success. Being able to give people value quickly and with little waste is a sign of success.

Transformational Leaders measures success based on Employee engagement, organisational commitment, innovation, and total performance improvements

How does technology help with Transformational Leadership?

Transformational leadership, a type of leadership that inspires and motivates followers to do great things, can be greatly improved by using technology in a smart way. Technology helps people communicate, work together, and come up with new ideas, which is in line with the main ideas of transformational leadership. The

Transformational Leadership method works better with the help of technology in these ways:

1. Digital communication platforms:

Transformational leaders use digital tools for communication, like messaging apps, videoconferencing, and teamwork tools, to make sure that everyone can talk to each other freely and openly. These platforms help leaders reach employees in different places, making sure that the organization's purpose and goals are communicated clearly and on time.

2. Data analytics and business intelligence:

Transformational leaders use business intelligence and data analytics tools to make smart choices. These technologies give leaders information about how well their companies are doing, how engaged their employees are, and what the market trends are. This information helps them make strategic choices that are in line with their company's vision.

3. Tools for working together and managing projects:

Transformational leaders use project management and collaboration platforms to encourage teamwork, new ideas, and fixing problems as a group. These technologies make it easier for teams to work together and give workers the freedom to share their ideas, learn from each other, and work towards shared goals.

4. Learning Management Systems (LMS) and Online Training:

Transformational leaders spend money on technology-based learning tools to help their employees keep learning. Learning Management Systems (LMS) and online training programmes make sure employees can access the right training materials. This encourages a culture of lifelong learning and personal growth.

5. Social Media and Employee Engagement Platforms:

Transformational leaders use social media and platforms for employee involvement to connect with employees, share the company's vision, and acknowledge each person's contributions. These tools make it easier for people to talk to each other openly and help the organisation feel more like a community.

What Analysis Says?

Technology is a key part of making the key traits of transformational leadership easier to do and better. Transformational leaders can make the workplace a place where creativity, open communication, and constant learning are encouraged by using digital communication platforms, data analytics, collaboration tools, online training, and social media. These technological tools help innovative leadership work better in the modern workplace as a whole.

Transformational Leadership in the Twenty-First Century:

A new type of leader is needed to successfully manage the challenges of Lean Digital Transformations, and this is the focus of the 2.0 version of transformational leadership. In addition to the standard methods of leadership, these leaders put an emphasis on the people involved in the change and foster an atmosphere where everyone may flourish.

Inspiring a Shared Vision: Transformational leaders inspire a shared vision by sharing the why, where, and how of the Lean Digital Transformation. They encourage others to take part in the change process by showing them how their individual efforts fit into the bigger vision.

Collaborative Trust-Building: Collaborative trust-building is a cornerstone of effective Lean Digital Transformations. Leaders who transform their followers' perspectives do so by creating a community where everyone feels safe sharing their thoughts and receiving constructive criticism. They make people feel secure enough to try new things, make mistakes, and improve.

Empowering and Developing People: Transformative leaders help their teams succeed by giving them more responsibility, more freedom, and more opportunities to learn and grow on the job. They spot potential in their employees, provide them with opportunities for advancement, and encourage a growth mindset among them.

Leading by Example: Transformational leaders set the standard for their teams' values, actions, and mindsets by exemplifying those traits themselves. They are hard workers who are also resilient, flexible, and dedicated to improving themselves professionally and personally.

Managing Change and Overcoming Resistance: Overcoming resistance to change is an important part of managing that change. Leaders that are capable of transformation recognise this and take measures to proactively manage change by reducing fears, involving followers in decision-making, and offering encouragement throughout the process. They aid in getting beyond resistance and developing a sense of ownership and dedication to the change.

The Value of People's Support

All levels of management must be invested in and supportive of a Lean Digital Transformation. The transformation efforts will face many difficulties, and they may even fail if people are not involved and supportive. Some people may not support the transition because they are worried about losing their jobs, because they are resistant to new ways of working, because they don't see the point in it, or because they are confused about what is happening.

In order to gain the support of their followers, transformative leaders must:

- Leaders must successfully communicate the Lean Digital Transformation's purpose, advantages, and desired results. A sense of community and mutual comprehension can be fostered if they respond to people's concerns and thoughtfully consider their suggestions.

- Leaders need to provide training and tools so that people can adjust to the new circumstances brought on by the transformation. This could be done through the provision of access to appropriate resources, such as training courses, mentorship, and coaching.

- It's important for leaders to cultivate an atmosphere where employees feel comfortable taking risks and sharing their ideas. Positive and supportive cultures that encourage participation and innovation can be fostered through the practise of recognising and rewarding effort and achievement.

- Leaders should get their followers invested in the outcome of decisions and invite their input whenever possible. Leaders can increase employees' buy-in to the change by soliciting their opinions and letting them participate in designing it.

- Leaders should frequently assess the development of the Lean Digital Transformation, providing comments and direction to people and groups as necessary. This is useful for acknowledging achievements and reiterating the significance of the transformational journey.

Lean Digital transformations can only be successful with the full buy-in and participation of all stakeholders. Leaders that understand the importance of this factor and make the happiness and participation of others a top priority are more likely to succeed in navigating the complexity of transformation and producing long-lasting results.

Key Takeaways

Jake Thompson's experience exemplifies the significance of the interplay among Lean concepts, digital technologies, and individuals in successful Lean Digital Transformations. Leaders who strive to make positive changes in their organisations know that they need more than technical know-how to make an impact. They also need soft skills to build trust, encourage healthy work-life balance, and give their employees a voice in the workplace.

Successful Lean Digital Transformations may be driven by transformational leaders that recognise the importance of and take steps to foster the connection between Lean, digital, and people.

4.6 Checklists for All Functions Leaders to Develop their Digital Capability

In the era of Lean Digital Transformation, it is crucial for businesses to understand that the digital function is not only responsible for the development of digital capabilities. Leaders in every industry and role must improve their digital skills if they are to successfully embrace digital transformation. In this section, we present checklists detailing five important talents that leaders across departments (such as Lean, Finance, Human Resources, Sales, and more) should prioritise developing during digital transformation. These skills will equip leaders of individual functions to contribute more effectively to the digital transformation effort as a whole within the organisation.

4.6.1 Digital Capability Development Checklists:

Lean Function:

- Gain the ability to map and analyse digital processes within the Lean framework. Learn how digital tools may be used to streamline processes, cut down on unnecessary steps, and boost productivity. Opportunities for digitalization and incremental enhancement can be discovered with the help of technologies like value stream mapping and process automation.

- Agile project management is a methodology and set of practises that may be used to successfully oversee digital transformation projects. Learn to deconstruct large projects into simpler ones and practise rapid iteration. Encourage teamwork, flexibility, and lifelong learning to advance the digitalization of Lean procedures.

- Learn data analytics skills for analysing digital data and metrics (Lean Data Analytics). Use performance monitoring, trend identification, and data-driven decision-making provided by digital analytics technologies. Make use of A/B testing and root cause analysis, two staples of lean data analytics, to push for change and improve the digital consumer experience.

- Digital Supply Chain Optimisation: Recognise how digital technologies have impacted the supply chain and create plans to enhance digital supply chain operations. Investigate technologies like blockchain, IoT, and cloud-based platforms to boost supply chain transparency, tracking, and teamwork.

- Create an environment where digital innovation and continuous improvement are encouraged inside the Lean function. Inspire your staff to take advantage of digital resources, try something new, and talk about what worked. Foster a growth mentality and offer staff training to help them adjust to new technologies.

Finance Function:

- Learn to make use of data analytics and digital tools to improve your financial forecasting and planning. Support strategic decision-making and increase the precision of forecasts through the application of cutting-edge financial modelling tools such as predictive analytics and scenario planning.

- Explore the use of automation and RPA (robotic process automation) in banking and financial services. Determine which time-consuming, error-prone manual processes may be automated instead. Learn to use process automation software and make sure it can communicate with your other digital systems.

- Learn about the state of data privacy and how to protect your personal information in the digital era. Create plans to safeguard confidential financial information, ensure financial compliance, and implement strong cybersecurity measures inside the finance department.

- Adopt digital financial reporting tools and technology to improve financial reporting's timeliness, accuracy, and transparency. Investigate the use of cloud-based reporting platforms, dynamic dashboards, and data visualisation technologies in order to effectively convey financial insights.

- Working together with vendors and other technology partners, investigate digital solutions that might drive financial transformation; this is the focus of strategic financial partnerships. Gain the skills to evaluate and negotiate strategic alliances, calculate the impact on the bottom line, and coordinate digital projects with overarching company objectives.

Human Resources Function:

- As part of HR's mission, you must build the infrastructure to effectively source, interview, and hire digital talent. To find and connect with people who have the necessary digital skills and talents, use online resources like social media and data analytics. Consider doing interviews and tests online to evaluate a candidate's comfort with technology.

- Set up digital learning programmes to reskill and train employees. Make use of microlearning modules, online learning platforms, and virtual training to ensure that your employees have access to ongoing education. Create digital leadership training programmes to foster the development of the company's future digital leaders.

- Make the Most of Digital Tools to Improve Employee Experience and Engagement! The feedback, recognition, and communication processes with employees should all be moved to digital platforms. Encourage teamwork and the exchange of ideas by implementing social intranets and other forms of online collaboration software.

- Workforce planning, talent management, and employee engagement can all benefit from a company's ability to analyse and interpret HR data. For effective strategic workforce planning, use HR analytics tools to see patterns, foresee employee turnover, and base choices on hard data.

- Automate HR procedures via self-service portals, chatbots, and cloud-based HRIS solutions. e. Digital HR Operations Free up HR time and energy for more strategic endeavours by streamlining administrative duties and providing digital access to HR services for employees.

Sales Function:

- For the Sales Department, Master the art of empowering your sales force with the latest and greatest digital tools and technologies. Put in place a CRM system to keep tabs on your customers, streamline your business procedures, and analyse your sales data. Support sales efforts with sales analytics, digital content, and team collaboration software.

- Omnichannel Sales Strategy: Recognise the value of an omnichannel sales approach and plan for the smooth fusion of offline and online channels. Increase customer involvement and revenues with the help of modern mediums like the Internet and mobile apps.

- Data-Driven Sales Insights: Learn to Dissect Sales Metrics for Meaningful Insights You can learn more about your customers' buying habits, find more sales opportunities, and tailor your approach by using sales analytics solutions. Use data analytics for forecasting sales patterns and better allocating resources.

- Sales and Marketing Alignment: Encourage communication and coordination between these two departments. Learn to communicate effectively about digital marketing, consumer segmentation, and lead generation. Measure the success of marketing initiatives and back up sales efforts with data from digital marketing analytics.

- Customer Relationship Management: Put the customer first and create digital tactics to strengthen your bonds with existing ones. Make use of customer relationship management software, automation, and personalization to provide memorable service to your clientele. Create the capacity to examine client information and make specific, relevant, and helpful suggestions.

Supply Chain Function:

- Digital Supply Chain Visibility: Develop the ability to utilise digital technologies like IoT sensors, RFID, and blockchain to achieve real-time visibility across the supply chain. Make use of data analytics in order to keep tabs on stock, gauge interest, streamline operations, and improve supply chain responsiveness.

- Agile and Collaborative Planning: Adopt agile planning approaches and encourage teamwork to adapt swiftly to shifting market needs. Improve supply chain coordination, demand prediction, and stock management with the help of digital platforms and solutions for communication across supply chain partners.

- Supply chain analytics: Gain expertise in supply chain analytics so you can use data to inform strategic decisions. Identify patterns, predict demand, and maximise stock by utilising predictive analytics and machine learning algorithms. Leverage analytics to drive supply chain continuous improvement projects.

- Digital Supplier Management: Optimise your supplier management procedures by using digital tools and platforms. Digital procurement systems, supplier portals, and automated performance tracking all contribute to greater efficiency and lower costs.

- Create the ability to recognise and counteract supply chain hazards through technological interventions. Improve the robustness of your supply chain through the use of analytics and simulation tools for risk assessment and management.

Safety Function:

- Real-Time Digital Safety Reporting and Monitoring: Safety may be monitored and reported in real time by using digital tools. Make use of Internet of Things (IoT) gadgets, wearable technologies, and digital sensors to monitor safety metrics, spot risks, and send timely alerts. To take preventative safety measures, use data analytics to spot patterns and trends.

- Virtual Training and Simulation: Safety training programmes can be improved by implementing virtual training and simulation technology. Make use of VR and AR technologies to give employees real safety simulations, engaging training materials, and mind-blowing experiences.

- Safety data analytics: build your skills in this area to find problem spots and propel preventative safety measures. Make use of data analytics to examine accident reports and safety checks for hidden dangers.

- Digital Safety Compliance: Safety compliance processes and documentation can be greatly simplified by adopting digital solutions. Safety inspections, audits, and reports on compliance should all be conducted and stored digitally. Safety requirements and regulations can be met with the help of automated compliance workflows.

- Safety Culture and Communication: Promote an organisation-wide digitally-enabled safety culture. Promote safety awareness, communicate best practises, and encourage employee engagement in safety efforts by using digital communication tools, including mobile applications, instant messaging, and collaborative platforms.

The Role of Customer Service:

- Providing an End-to-End Customer Journey: Build the capacity to provide a consistent, individualised digital consumer experience across all touchpoints. Improve client engagement and happiness with the use of a customer relationship management (CRM) system, chatbots, and self-service portals.

- Enhancing Customer Engagement: Use data analytics and other digital resources to learn as much as possible about your customers. To learn about consumers' likes, dislikes, and suggestions, use customer data platforms, social media listening tools, and sentiment analysis. Improve consumer relationships by customising your service or product for each individual.

- Agile Service Delivery: Use agile approaches to meet the changing needs of your customers swiftly. Create interdisciplinary groups with the authority to resolve customer complaints, use technology to solve problems quickly, and launch quality-improvement campaigns to boost customer service.

- Proactive Customer Support: Anticipate client demands and give proactive help through the use of digital technologies like predictive analytics and AI-powered chatbots. To guarantee prompt and effective customer support, automated methods for problem tracking, resolution, and escalation must be put into place.

- Continuous Service Improvement: Improve customer service by encouraging a mindset of constant refining and evolution (i.e., "continuous service improvement"). To determine where your service may be improved, you should use customer surveys, analytics, and other forms of digital feedback. Use data analytics software to track key performance indicators and motivate your team towards consistently excellent customer service.

Quality Function:

- In order to streamline quality procedures, paperwork, and compliance, it is important for the quality function to make use of digital quality management systems. To maintain high quality standards over time, use digital audit tools, automated workflows, and cloud-based quality management platforms.

- Develop skills in data analytics and statistical process control to keep an eye on and understand quality data. b. Data-Driven Quality Monitoring To spot changes in quality and set in motion remedial measures, use digital technologies for continuous data collection, process monitoring, and analysis.

- Adopt digital technology like Internet of Things (IoT) sensors and automation to improve quality control procedures. To guarantee product and procedure conformity, use digital inspection tools, automated testing, and data analytics.

- Create digital capabilities for efficient supplier quality management. Get your suppliers on board with digital tools for monitoring their performance, checking their quality, and working together. In order to evaluate the quality of your suppliers and push for constant advancement in the supply chain, you need to use data analytics.

- Encourage a mindset of constant refinement and advancement in the name of quality. Take advantage of technology tools for effective staff communication, participation, and coordination. Take advantage of digital resources for performing root-cause analysis, implementing remedial steps, and taking preventative measures.

Business Case Example

XYZ Corporation - A Digital Transformation Success Story

As part of its digital transformation, the multinational manufacturing firm XYZ Corporation pushed for the enhancement of digital skills across all departments. The company realised that digital transformation needed input and participation from all departments, not just the digital one. The extraordinary success of XYZ Corporation can be attributed to the incorporation of the following talents across all departments:

Supply Chain: Digital supply chain visibility was deployed at XYZ Company, allowing for constant stock counts, demand checks, and logistical improvements. Increased customer satisfaction and less downtime were the results of this change in the supply chain's responsiveness and lead times.

Safety: With the use of Internet of Things (IoT) sensors and data analytics, XYZ Company has embraced digital safety monitoring and reporting to proactively identify and eliminate threats. They improved the effectiveness of safety training and decreased the number of workplace mishaps by adopting virtual training and simulation technologies.

Customer Service: In order to create a consistent and individualised experience for its clientele, XYZ Corporation's customer service department adopted an omnichannel customer experience strategy, incorporating customer relationship management (CRM) software, chatbots, and self-service portals. Because of this, we were able to boost our brand's reputation, client satisfaction, and loyalty.

Quality: The XYZ Company has implemented data-driven quality monitoring and digital quality management systems to ensure product consistency. They were able to accomplish better quality standards, decrease faults, and enhance product quality by using digital technologies for real-time data collection and analysis.

Finances: To make better predictions and use data to make decisions, XYZ Company implemented digital financial planning and analysis tools. Financial processes have been automated and roboticized to cut down on human error and increase productivity.

The previously mentioned skills enabled XYZ Corporation's successful digital transformation, which resulted in improved operational performance, cost savings, and increased competitiveness.

4.6.2 Functions Capabilities during Digital Transformation

For an organisation to undergo a true digital transformation, digital capabilities must be built up throughout all departments. The following table provides checklists for several key business processes that leaders should prioritise throughout digital transformation. These processes include Lean, Supply Chain, Purchase, Quality, Sales, Human resources, Finance, Safety, and Customer Service.

Table 1: Functional Capability

Function	Capability 1	Capability 2	Capability 3	Capability 4	Capability 5	Capability 6
Lean	Value Stream Mapping and Analysis	Lean Process Automation	Continuous Improvement Culture	Visual Management and Performance Tracking	Data-Driven Decision Making	Lean Six Sigma Methodology
Supply Chain	Digital Supply Chain Visibility	Agile and Collaborative Planning	Supply Chain Analytics	Digital Supplier Management	Supply Chain Resilience and Risk Management	Demand Sensing and Forecasting
Purchase	Digital Supplier Onboarding	E-Procurement and E-Sourcing	Spend Analysis and Cost Optimization	Contract Management and Automation	Supplier Relationship Management	Supplier Performance Tracking
Quality	Digital Quality Management Systems	Data-Driven Quality Monitoring	Digital Quality Assurance	Supplier Quality Management	Continuous Quality Improvement	Statistical Process Control
Sales	CRM Implementation and Integration	Digital Sales Enablement and Automation	Customer Data Analytics	Sales Performance Tracking and Analysis	Personalized Customer Experience	Sales Forecasting and Pipeline Management
Human Resource	Digital Talent Acquisition	HR Analytics and Data-Driven Insights	Employee Self-Service and Automation	Digital Learning and Development	Performance Management Systems	Employee Engagement Platforms
Finance	Digital Financial Planning and Analysis	Automation and Robotics	Data-Driven Decision Making	Digital Compliance and Risk Management	Integration with Digital Platforms	Real-Time Financial Reporting
Safety	Digital Safety Monitoring and Reporting	Virtual Training and Simulation	Safety Data Analytics	Digital Safety Compliance	Safety Culture and Communication	Incident Reporting and Investigation
Customer Service	Omni-Channel Customer Experience	Digital Customer Insights	Agile Service Delivery	Proactive Customer Support	Continuous Service Improvement	Customer Service Analytics

Leaders in all areas of an organisation should make improving their digital competence a top priority if they are to successfully lead their companies through the digital transformation.

Acquiring digital skills and expertise, encouraging a culture of digital innovation, welcoming emerging technologies, and fostering collaboration and cross-functional collaborations are all important items on a checklist for leaders to enhance their digital competence.

Leaders can help themselves and their teams become more digitally capable by constantly learning, keeping up with digital developments, and looking for ways to utilise digital strategies and technologies in their work.

Chapter Summary

In "Focus Three: It's a People Game—Why is it Everyone's Responsibility?" we go into the significance of shared accountability in the context of Lean Digital transformation. This chapter explores a wide range of topics, including the drawbacks of working in silos, the skillsets required of Lean Digital leaders, an appreciation for agility, the importance of transformational leadership, the debut of the Lean Digital Transformation Model (TL 2.0), and checklists to help leaders improve their digital prowess.

- The chapter stresses the necessity of removing obstacles and encouraging communication between teams and departments, arguing that Lean Digital cannot flourish in isolation.

- Having a firm grasp of Lean principles, digital technology, leadership skills, the capacity to effectively communicate, and the fortitude to deal with complexity are just a few of the critical attributes Lean Digital leaders should have, as highlighted in this chapter.

- This chapter challenges readers to consider if they have a firm grasp of the notion of "agile" and its implications for themselves and their organisations in today's fast-paced business world.

- This chapter emphasises the importance of transformational leaders and how they may drive successful Lean Digital transformation projects by fostering a culture of continuous improvement and innovation through their capacity to inspire and motivate their teams.

- The TL 2.0 Model: This chapter presents the Lean Digital Transformation Model (TL 2.0), informing readers about the model and how it differs from more conventional methods of transformation and giving a framework for carrying out successful Lean Digital Transformation projects.

- With the help of the chapter's checklists, leaders in a wide range of fields and roles can improve their digital competence and prepare themselves to take advantage of emerging opportunities.

Key Questions for Readers 

1. Why is it critical for Lean Digital projects to encourage cross-departmental cooperation and eliminate silos? When working in silos, what problems can arise, and how can companies encourage teamwork?

2. What are the most important skills that should be possessed by leaders in the Lean Digital space? What role do these skills play in the success of Lean Digital transformation efforts, and how can leaders improve these skills?

3. In today's fast-paced, ever-changing corporate climate, do individuals really grasp the meaning and significance of agility? What are the most important characteristics of an agile person or team, and what can businesses and individuals do to develop these traits?

4. For what reasons are visionary leaders crucial to Lean Digital initiatives? How can transformational leaders achieve effective digital transformation inside their organisations, and what special qualities and talents do they bring to the table?

5. How does one define TL 2.0, or the Lean Digital Transformation Model? What makes it unique from other kinds of models of change, and what exactly does it consist of? How can businesses use this model to efficiently implement Lean Digital transformation?

6. How can leaders in various fields improve their digital skills? What kinds of criteria or recommendations can they use? When it comes to their respective areas of expertise, how can leaders best improve their digital literacy and proficiency?

Part Five

Focus Four: Technology is Process Enabler only

Why 90% Digital Transformation fails?

"However beautiful the strategy, you should occasionally look at the results."

~Winston Churchill

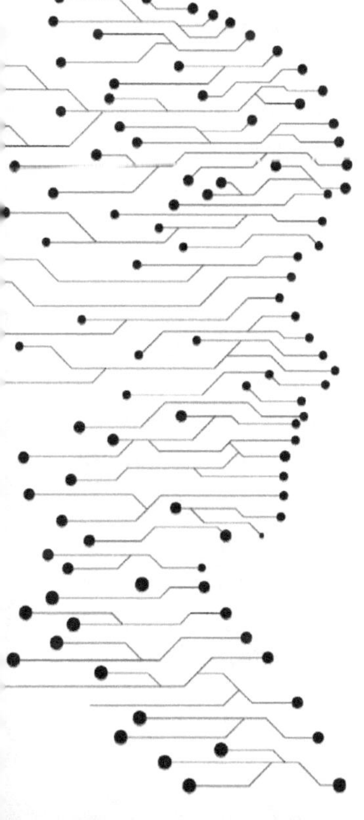

Figure 10: Major Digital Lean Challenges

In the previous chapter we have seen what digital transformation is and what it is not. It is a journey and it's not all about technology. Although it uses technology to fundamentally transform the way organizations think about and approach their business processes, customer interactions, and employee experiences.

Some of those who experienced failure with the adoption of lean and digital transformation did because they failed to focus on people and culture. They also lack cross-functional collaboration, and over-rely on Technology. The current trends reveals that lean and digital transformation needs visionary leaders who have a transformational mindset to lead this development.

In a competitive corporate environment, one organisation decided to undergo a digital transformation. They had heard about the fantastic results that could be achieved through Lean Digital practises, such as greater productivity and better interactions with customers. They decided to use this new method since they were enthusiastic about its potential. They didn't realise that the trials would test their endurance just as much as the benefits.

Internal opposition was the first problem they had to deal with. It's true that change might be difficult to accept. Employees were hesitant to adopt new technology and approaches since they were used to working with the status quo. In order to overcome this obstacle, the corporation knew that it needed to implement a change management strategy. They put money into training programmes, workshops, and coaching sessions to help employees gain comfort with and appreciation for the advantages of Lean Digital transformation.

The use of outdated technology and legacy systems also posed a problem. The company's attempts at digital transformation were hindered by the constraints of its current technology stack. They were making slow progress due to integration problems, data silos, and incompatible platforms, which could have derailed their transformation effort altogether. The organisation adopted digital platforms that were both scalable and flexible, updated their infrastructure, and implemented strong integration solutions to meet this problem.

They ran into new trouble with cybersecurity. The company's exposure to cyberattacks increased as it embraced digital technologies. Security methods and procedures had to be significantly tightened up. They collaborated extensively with cybersecurity specialists to strengthen their digital defences, guaranteeing the safety of their customers' data and other sensitive information throughout the transition.

The lack of necessary skills was another obstacle the organisation had to overcome. They realised they were missing key personnel with the knowledge and skills to effectively exploit the benefits of Lean Digital strategies. They implemented extensive upskilling and reskilling programmes to close the gap and equip their workforce to successfully push the change forward.

Throughout its development, the business received encouragement and guidance from a variety of sources. Experts in the field of Lean Digital transformation were contacted, including Mary Poppendieck and Eric Ries. They looked at studies written by members of the Lean Enterprise Institute and McKinsey & Company, as well as case studies from companies that had accomplished similar changes.

Challenges were not barriers to growth but rather stepping stones to success as the organisation moved along the path of Lean Digital transformation. Their determination and appreciation for the revolutionary potential of Lean Digital practises grew stronger with each challenge they surmounted.

Digital transformation is a complex process that requires organizations to adopt new technologies, processes, and ways of working to stay competitive in the modern business environment. However, despite the potential benefits of digital transformation, many orgasnizations fail to achieve the desired results. In fact, research suggests that up to 90% of digital transformation initiatives fail to deliver the expected outcomes. In this section, we will explore some of the challenges that organizations face when implementing digital transformation initiatives in a lean environment.

These challenges include:

1. Lack of Leadership Alignment:

One of the most common challenges we have seen organizations face is a lack of alignment among leadership teams. Without clear and consistent leadership, digital transformation initiatives are unlikely to succeed. Leaders must be committed to the process and have a shared vision for what they hope to achieve. They should also be willing to invest time and resources in the initiative.

2. Data Management:

The sheer volume of data that is generated by digital technologies can be difficult to manage and analyze effectively. Businesses must have robust data management strategies and processes in place to make sense of this data and turn it into actionable insights. This includes having the right tools and technologies for collecting, storing, and analyzing data, as well as the skills and expertise to interpret and use that data effectively.

Moreover, data privacy is a critical concern for businesses operating in the digital age. With the increasing frequency of data breaches and cyber attacks, businesses must ensure that they comply with data privacy regulations and protect their customers' data from unauthorized access or use. Failure to do so can result in significant financial and reputational damage, as well as legal penalties. Therefore, data management is a crucial challenge that organizations must overcome to achieve digital lean success.

3. Siloed Organizational Structures:

Another challenge that organizations face is the presence of siloed organizational structures. In many organizations, different departments or business units work independently of one another, making it difficult to share information, collaborate, and make decisions quickly. This siloed approach can hinder digital transformation initiatives as they require cross-functional collaboration and communication. It can also lead to duplication of efforts, inefficient use of resources, and slow decision-making, which can delay the implementation of digital solutions.

4. Lack of Digital Maturity:

Digital transformation requires a level of digital maturity, meaning that an organization has a comprehensive understanding of digital technologies and how they can be utilized to improve their business processes. This can be a significant challenge for businesses that have not invested in digital technologies in the past and lack the internal resources and expertise required to adopt new digital tools. It's important to note that this challenge is more prevalent in traditional industries that have been slow to embrace digital technologies. These industries include manufacturing, construction, and logistics, among others.

In these industries, the lack of digital maturity is often attributed to the fact that many of their business processes have been standardized over decades, if not centuries, and is heavily reliant on manual labor and physical assets. For example, in the manufacturing industry, production lines have been designed around human operators, and the use of robotics and automation is still in its early stages.

5. Legacy Systems and Processes:

Many organizations have legacy systems and processes that are not designed for a digital environment. Legacy systems and processes refer to the outdated technology and processes that businesses have been using for a long time. These systems may have been effective in the past, but they may not be suitable for the digital age. With the adoption of new digital technologies, businesses need to adapt their legacy systems and processes to keep up with the changing trends.

Legacy systems and processes can be a significant challenge for digital transformation initiatives. It is difficult to integrate new digital technologies with old legacy systems that were not designed to work together. The lack of interoperability between these systems can lead to inefficiencies and duplication of efforts. The cost and time required to update these systems can be significant, making it difficult for businesses to justify the investment.

6. The Difficulty of Changing the Company Culture:

Many organizations have been operating under the same traditional culture for years, and it can be challenging to convince employees to embrace change. In some cases, employees may even resist the change and see it as a threat to their jobs, leading to a lack of cooperation, slow adoption, and ultimately, failure.

7. Implementation Process can be Costly and Time-consuming:

Implementing new technologies and processes can require significant investments in terms of both money and time. It can also disrupt existing operations, leading to a loss of productivity during the transition period. As a result, some companies may be hesitant to pursue digital lean initiatives due to the perceived costs and risks associated with it.

8. Ensuring that the Technology being Used is Aligned with the Overall Business Strategy:

Many companies make the mistake of investing in technology without fully understanding how it fits into their business objectives. This can result in the adoption of technology that does not provide the expected benefits or fails to address the organization's most significant pain points.

9. Cybersecurity Risks:

The integration of digital technologies exposes organizations to new cybersecurity risks. Digital transformation initiatives can create new vulnerabilities that could be exploited by cybercriminals, and it is essential for businesses to have robust cybersecurity measures in place to mitigate these risks.

Key Takeaways

To overcome these challenges, businesses must develop a robust digital transformation strategy that incorporates lean methodology. It is important to prioritize initiatives that align with the organization's goals and objectives and to engage all stakeholders in the process. Businesses must also invest in the necessary resources, such as technology and personnel, to ensure successful implementation of digital transformation initiatives.

One example of a company that has successfully integrated digital transformation with lean methodology is Toyota. The company has implemented a range of digital tools, such as automation and artificial intelligence, to streamline its manufacturing processes and improve efficiency. By adopting lean principles, such as continuous improvement and waste reduction, Toyota has been able to leverage digital technologies to achieve significant cost savings and improved productivity.

5.2 Digitization Vs Digitalization Vs Digital Transformation Vs Lean Digital

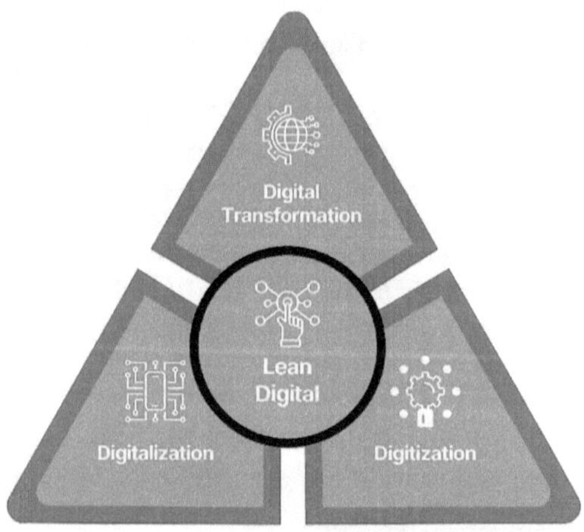

Figure 11: Digitization Vs Digitalization Vs Digital Transformation Vs Lean Digital

In the context of digital transformation and business, the terms digitization and digitalization are often used interchangeably, but they actually refer to different processes. Some even refer to digital transformation as digitalization, and some are far from understanding what Lean Digital is. In this chapter, we have an overview of what each one of them is, thus we wll be able to tell the difference between the four concepts.

Digitization

Digitization is the process of converting analog information into digital format, allowing it to be processed, stored, and transmitted electronically. This can include scanning paper documents, converting analog audio or video recordings into digital files, or creating digital versions of physical products.

One practical example of digitization that you would have seen is the digitization of medical records. In the past, medical records were typically kept on paper and stored in filing cabinets, making it difficult to share information between healthcare providers and creating the risk of lost or damaged records. By digitizing medical records, healthcare providers can easily access patient information from any location, allowing for better collaboration and faster decision-making.

Digitization of manufacturing processes is another prominent example of digitization. This include the use of digital design tools to create product models, the use of sensors and data analysis tools to monitor production processes in real-time, and the use of 3D printing to create physical products from digital models. Digitization can help manufacturers improve product quality, reduce waste, and increase efficiency.

Digitalization

Digitalization is the process of integrating digital technologies into various aspects of business operations to enhance efficiency, productivity, and customer satisfaction. This involves the use of digital tools such as automation, cloud computing, big data analytics, and the Internet of Things (IoT) to digitize manual or paper-based processes. Digitalization enables businesses to optimize their operations, reduce costs, and create new business models. It also enhances the customer experience by providing better and more personalized services.

Digital Transformation

The term "digital transformation" refers to a comprehensive and strategic change in an organization's values, policies, procedures, and business models in order to make full use of digital technologies. The entire value chain, customer experience, and market standing need to be rethought. As an illustration, Uber has shaken up the cab industry by creating a mobile app that connects customers with drivers.

Changes in the publishing industry brought on by the popularity of e-books, web-based authoring tools, and digital content delivery.

Examples of digital transformation initiatives include the use of artificial intelligence and machine learning to analyze customer data and deliver personalized experiences, the implementation of cloud computing to improve data storage and access, and the adoption of digital marketing techniques to reach a wider audience.

One example of a successful digital transformation initiative is the mobile banking app developed by Ally Bank. The app allows customers to manage their accounts, deposit checks, and transfer money all from their mobile devices. The app has been praised for its user-friendly design and convenience, resulting in increased customer satisfaction and loyalty.

Another example is the digital transformation of General Electric (GE). The company implemented a new digital strategy, which involved the use of big data analytics, cloud computing, and the Internet of Things (IoT) to improve its business processes and deliver better products and services. As a result of this transformation, GE was able to reduce costs, improve productivity, and increase revenue.

Lean Digital

Lean Digital is a management philosophy that combines the principles of Lean Manufacturing with the opportunities presented by digital technologies. It aims to improve organizational agility, innovation, and customer-centricity, while reducing waste and inefficiency.

The Lean Digital approach involves the continuous improvement of processes, products, and services through rapid experimentation and iteration, based on feedback from customers and stakeholders. It emphasizes the use of data and analytics to inform decision-making, and the development of a culture of learning and collaboration.

Organizations that adopt the Lean Digital approach typically use cross-functional teams and agile methodologies to rapidly develop and test new products and services, and to respond to changing market conditions. They also prioritize customer experience and engagement, and seek to leverage digital technologies to create new and better ways of delivering value to customers.

One of the key benefits of the Lean Digital approach is that it allows organizations to be nimbler and more responsive in the face of rapid technological change and shifting customer expectations. It also helps organizations to identify and eliminate wasteful practices, leading to greater efficiency and cost savings. To successfully implement Lean Digital, organizations should focus on building a culture of continuous improvement, investing in digital skills training, and leveraging agile methodologies and digital tools.

Differentiating between digitization, digitalization, digital transformation, and Lean Digital is essential in the fields of technology and business. Each of these phrases describes a unique strategy for leveraging technological resources and improving operational efficiency.

5.2.1 Here are some practical examples of how you can use digitalization?

- **Electronic Document Management:** Many companies are switching from paper-based systems to electronic document management systems, which allow for faster and more efficient document sharing, storage, and retrieval. For example, the healthcare industry has adopted electronic health records (EHRs) to streamline patient information management.

- **Digital Marketing:** Companies are using digital marketing techniques such as search engine optimization (SEO), social media marketing, and email marketing to reach customers and improve their online presence. For example, Amazon uses personalized email marketing to suggest products to customers based on their browsing history.

- **Automation:** Automation tools like chatbots, robotic process automation (RPA), and machine learning algorithms are being used to automate repetitive and time-consuming tasks, reducing errors and improving efficiency. For example, the banking industry has adopted chatbots to provide customer support and automate routine banking tasks.

- **Internet of Things (IoT):** IoT refers to the integration of devices, sensors, and machines to collect and analyze data, improve processes, and optimize performance. For example, the manufacturing industry is using IoT sensors to monitor equipment performance and predict maintenance needs.

To illustrate the difference between digitization and digitalization, think about a retail store. Digitization in this context might involve scanning paper receipts and storing them digitally, making it easier to search for and retrieve them when needed. Digitalization, on the other hand, might involve implementing a mobile app that allows customers to browse and purchase products online, using data analytics to understand customer preferences, and using automation technologies to optimize inventory management and order fulfillment.

5.2.2 The Differences amongst Digitization, Digitalization, Digital Transformation and Lean Digital

Here are five main distinctions between them:

Scope: The primary goal of digitization is to transform analogue data into digital formats, while the primary goal of digitalization is to incorporate digital tools into preexisting processes. Lean Digital blends lean management principles with digital transformation activities, which is necessary because digital transformation necessitates a drastic shift in strategy.

Objectives: The goal of digitising information is to make it easier to access and store. The primary goals of digitalization are to improve productivity and decision-making. The goal of digital transformation is to completely rethink the value chain and the way customers interact with a company. The goal of "Lean Digital" is zero waste and constant enhancement of processes.

Cultural Impact: Organisational culture will undergo profound shifts as a result of digital transformation. The cultural impact of Lean Digital may be less severe because it builds on established lean management practises.

Customer Focus: The focus of both digital transformation and Lean Digital is on the customer. However, the priorities of Lean Digital, particularly those centred on eliminating waste and improving efficiency, are more in tune with what consumers want.

Implementation Approach: Digitization and Digitalization are processes that typically require incremental improvements and apply nicely to smaller projects. More extensive organisational changes and strategic planning are needed for digital transformation and Lean Digital.

Key Takeaways

In a Lean Digital environment, both digitization and digitalization can play important roles. Digitization can help to eliminate waste and streamline processes, while digitalization can help to create new value and drive innovation.

By understanding the distinction between these two concepts, businesses can develop more effective digital transformation strategies and achieve greater success in their efforts to become more digitally mature.

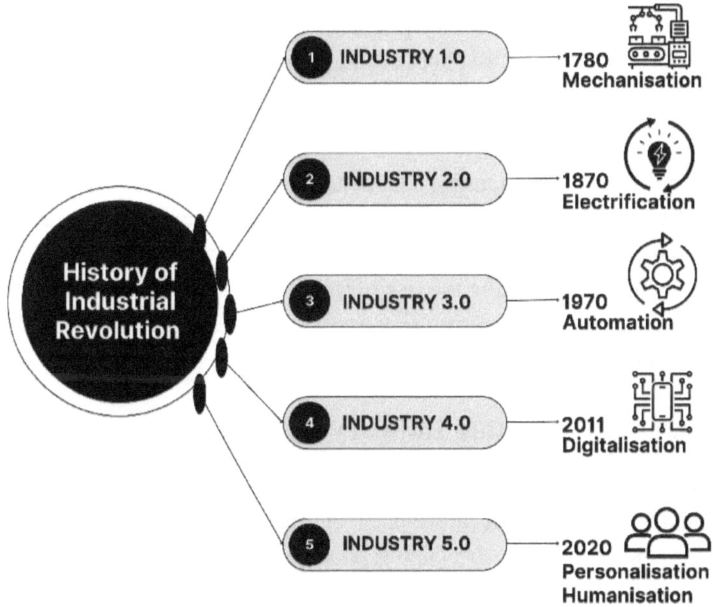

Figure 12: Industry 5.0 Revolution

5.3.1 What is Industry 5.0?

Industry 5.0 is a term that has been recently introduced to the manufacturing industry, which represents the next phase of industrial development. This new industry concept builds upon the principles of Industry 4.0 and aims to address some of the challenges posed by the previous stages of industrial revolution which include:

Industry 1.0: The first industrial revolution was characterized by the use of steam power and mechanization to improve productivity.

Industry 2.0: The second industrial revolution introduced mass production techniques, assembly lines, and the widespread use of electricity to power machinery.

Industry 3.0: The third industrial revolution, also known as the digital revolution, saw the introduction of computerization and automation to manufacturing processes.

Industry 4.0: The fourth industrial revolution, also known as the smart factory, saw the integration of digital technologies such as the Internet of Things (IoT), artificial intelligence (AI), and big data analytics into manufacturing processes.

Industry 5.0: It is seen as the next stage in this evolution, and it is characterized by the integration of human creativity and problem-solving skills with advanced automation and AI technologies. It aims to create a more collaborative and flexible manufacturing environment that can adapt quickly to changing customer needs and market demands. This collaboration between human and machines can improve the speed and quality of production, while also promoting creativity, problem-solving, and flexibility.

Some of the key features of Industry 5.0 include the use of collaborative robots, augmented and virtual reality, and the integration of sensors and other technologies into wearable devices. These tools can help workers to complete tasks more quickly and accurately, while also reducing the risk of injury or fatigue. The result is a more efficient and productive manufacturing process that can adapt to changing demands and market conditions.

5.3.2 Challenges to Adopting Industry 5.0

Industry 5.0, being a nascent concept, poses several challenges to its adoption. Some of the significant challenges include a lack of digital infrastructure and skilled workforce, high implementation costs, integration with legacy systems, resistance to change from employees and management, and security concerns.

- **Lack of Digital Infrastructure and Skilled Workforce**

One of the critical factors hindering the implementation of Industry 5.0 is the lack of digital infrastructure and skilled workforce. The manufacturing industry needs advanced technology such as robotics, IoT, AI, and big data analytics, which require digital infrastructure and highly skilled professionals. Unfortunately, many countries and companies have not invested sufficiently in the digital infrastructure and workforce development needed to support Industry 5.0.

- **High Implementation Costs**

Another significant challenge is the high implementation costs. Industry 5.0 requires significant investments in advanced technology, software, and training. As a result, many small and medium-sized companies may not be able to afford to implement Industry 5.0.

- **Integration with Legacy Systems**

Integrating Industry 5.0 with legacy systems is another major challenge. Many manufacturing companies still use legacy systems, which are not compatible with Industry 5.0 technologies. As a result, companies may need to replace or modify their existing systems to adopt Industry 5.0, which could be costly and time-consuming.

- **Resistance to Change from Employees and Management**

Resistance to change is also a significant challenge to the adoption of Industry 5.0. The introduction of new technology often requires changes in the organization's culture, processes, and management practices, which can be difficult to implement. Furthermore, employees may resist adopting new technologies because of the perceived threat to their jobs or the fear of not being able to use the new technology effectively.

- **Security Concerns**

Finally, security concerns are also a challenge to the adoption of Industry 5.0. The increased use of technology and connectivity in Industry 5.0 creates new vulnerabilities that could be exploited by cybercriminals. Companies need to develop effective cybersecurity measures to protect their operations and data.

5.3.3 Industry 5.0 Case Studies

There are several companies that have already begun implementing Industry 5.0 principles into their operations. One such example is Siemens, which has created a "digital twin" of its production facilities to simulate various scenarios and optimize operations. This has resulted in improved efficiency and reduced downtime. Another example is Bosch, which has implemented smart factory technologies that allow for real-time monitoring and predictive maintenance. This has resulted in significant cost savings and increased productivity.

Additionally, Chinese company Haier has implemented a "microenterprise" model, where teams of employees are responsible for their own products and processes within the larger organization. This decentralized approach has resulted in increased agility and innovation, as well as improved customer satisfaction.

These case studies demonstrate the potential benefits of Industry 5.0, but also highlight the need for significant investment in digital infrastructure and workforce training. Companies that have successfully implemented Industry 5.0 have often done so through a combination of technology implementation, organizational restructuring, and employee education and training.

5.3.4 Is Industry 5.0 Ready to Go?

Despite these challenges, there are many companies that have successfully implemented Industry 5.0 technologies. For example, German company **Robert Bosch GmbH** has developed a "smart factory" in China that incorporates Industry 5.0 technologies such as robotics and machine learning. Another example is BMW, which uses a "digital twin" system to simulate and optimize its production processes.

Looking to the future, it is likely that Industry 5.0 adoption will continue to grow as companies seek to remain competitive and meet customer demands for increased efficiency and customization. However, it will require a concerted effort from companies, governments, and educational institutions to address the challenges and ensure that the necessary infrastructure, skills, and resources are in place to support widespread adoption.

The readiness of industries to adopt Industry 5.0 varies depending on the industry, the country, and the company's size and culture. While some industries and companies are already implementing Industry 5.0, others are still in the early stages of Industry 4.0 adoption, and some are yet to embrace any digital transformation. However, the increasing awareness of Industry 5.0's potential benefits and the advancement of technology will drive its adoption in the future.

Key Takeaways

Industry 5.0 is a promising development for the manufacturing industry, emphasizing the importance of the human factor and advanced technologies.

The challenges to its adoption are significant but not insurmountable, and companies can learn from successful case studies and utilize best practices to overcome them.

The readiness of industries to adopt Industry 5.0 varies, but the trend towards digital transformation and the growing awareness of its benefits suggest that Industry 5.0 is indeed ready to go.

5.4 Examples of Successful Digital Road Maps from Other Successful Organizations

A lot of companies are rushing to adopt new technologies to remain competitive in this fast paced digital world. However, there having failures here and there, as you yourself might have encounter some challenges. A key reason for this failure is the lack of a clear and effective digital road map. A digital road map is a comprehensive plan that outlines a company's digital transformation journey, including the goals, milestones, and strategies needed to achieve those goals.

To create a successful digital road map, companies can learn from the experiences of others who have undergone a successful digital transformation.

By studying the digital road maps of successful organizations, companies can gain insights into the strategies and tactics that work best for their industry and business model. This can help them avoid common pitfalls and develop a more effective plan for their own digital transformation.

Here, we will explore examples of successful digital road maps from other organizations, analyzing their strategies and outcomes. lessons leant from these organizations can be applied to our own digital road maps, thereby increasing our chances of success and ensuring that we remain competitive in the ever-evolving digital landscape.

5.4.1 Examples of Successful Digital Road maps

Example 1: Amazon

Amazon's digital transformation journey is one of the most widely recognized and successful examples of a company adopting digital technologies to transform their business. The company's digital road map was centered on customer-centricity, data-driven decision-making, and agile methodology.

Amazon's focus on customer-centricity is reflected in their mission statement, "to be Earth's most customer-centric company." To achieve this, Amazon has used digital technologies to personalize the customer experience, offering tailored recommendations based on customer data and providing seamless checkout processes. Additionally, Amazon has used data analytics to track customer behavior and preferences, allowing them to make informed decisions about product offerings and pricing.

Another key aspect of Amazon's digital road map is their emphasis on data-driven decision-making. The company has invested heavily in data analytics and machine learning, using data to drive everything from product development to marketing campaigns. By leveraging data to make informed decisions, Amazon has been able to stay ahead of the competition and identify new opportunities for growth.

Finally, Amazon has also embraced agile methodology as part of their digital transformation strategy. Agile methodology is a project management approach that emphasizes flexibility and adaptability, allowing teams to respond quickly to changing market conditions and customer needs. By adopting agile methodology, Amazon has been able to develop new products and services at a rapid pace, giving them a significant competitive advantage.

The outcomes of Amazon's digital transformation have been nothing short of impressive. The company's revenue has grown from $34 billion in 2010 to over $386 billion in 2020, and they now employ over 1.3 million people worldwide. Amazon's success can be attributed in large part to their ability to leverage digital technologies to drive innovation and growth.

Example 2: Netflix

Netflix is a leading streaming platform that has undergone a successful digital transformation in recent years. Their digital road map prioritized personalization, innovation, and continuous improvement to stay ahead of their competitors and maintain their position as the industry leader.

Netflix's focus on personalization is evident in their data-driven approach to content curation. They use algorithms to analyze viewer behavior and preferences to recommend personalized content to each user. This approach has increased customer engagement and retention, as viewers feel that the platform understands their preferences and offers them relevant content.

In terms of innovation, Netflix has consistently pushed the boundaries of what is possible with streaming technology. They were early adopters of cloud computing, which allowed them to scale their platform rapidly and deliver a seamless streaming experience. They have also invested heavily in creating original content, which has helped them to differentiate their platform from competitors and attract new subscribers.

Finally, Netflix's commitment to continuous improvement has helped them to stay ahead of the curve in the rapidly-evolving streaming industry. They regularly test new features and functionalities, and use customer feedback to refine their platform and deliver a better user experience.

Example 3: Walmart

Walmart is a prime example of a traditional brick-and-mortar retailer that has successfully navigated the digital transformation landscape. In recent years, Walmart has made significant strides in integrating digital technologies into their business model to enhance their customer experience and streamline operations.

One of the key elements of Walmart's digital transformation road map has been its focus on omnichannel retail. By integrating their physical stores with their online presence, Walmart has created a seamless shopping experience for customers across all channels. For instance, customers can now order products online and pick them up at a nearby store, or have them delivered directly to their doorstep. This approach has enabled Walmart to leverage the strengths of both their physical and digital assets, resulting in increased customer satisfaction and loyalty.

Another crucial aspect of Walmart's digital transformation has been its efforts to optimize its supply chain through the use of digital technologies. Walmart has invested heavily in big data analytics and machine learning algorithms to help manage inventory levels and forecast demand. This has allowed them to reduce costs associated with overstocking and understocking products, and improve their overall supply chain efficiency.

Walmart has also embraced the use of emerging technologies, such as virtual reality and augmented reality, to enhance the customer experience. For instance, they have developed a virtual shopping assistant that uses augmented reality to help customers visualize how products would look in their home before making a purchase.

Example 4: General Electric (GE)

GE has started down the road to digital transformation with its "Digital Industrial" strategy. Their main strategy was to leverage the IIoT to link their machines, data, and analytics. GE optimised operations and enabled predictive maintenance for their industrial equipment by integrating sensors and gathering real-time data from their assets.

Example 5: Starbucks

Starbucks has created a digital road map with the goal of improving the customer experience via mobile devices. Mobile ordering, payments, and individualised rewards were all on their plan. Starbucks invested heavily in their mobile app and integrated it with their physical outlets to revolutionise the way people order and pay for their favourite beverages.

Example 6: Adidas

To improve customer interaction and tailor digital experiences to each individual, Adidas set out on a "digital roadmap." They invested money in e-commerce platforms, wearable fitness trackers, and virtual fitting rooms. With the help of technology, Adidas gave their customers new ways to engage with the company, create unique goods, and get in shape.

Example 7: Delta Air Lines

Delta Air Lines established a digital roadmap to revolutionise the consumer experience in the airline business. They planned to invest money in things like flight tracking applications, self-service kiosks, and smartphone apps. Delta improved customer service, accelerated the check-in procedure, and kept them informed of any delays or changes via digital technologies.

Example 8: Ford Motor Company

The Ford Motor Company has created a digital strategy that emphasises mobility and connected vehicles. They concentrated on incorporating cutting-edge technologies such as self-driving cars, battery-powered automobiles, and internet connectivity. Ford's goal in embracing digital transformation was to revolutionise transportation in the future and make cars safer and more enjoyable to use.

Example 9: Unilever

Unilever's digital plan sought to revamp the company's sustainability efforts and supply chain processes. They implemented blockchain and other technologies to increase supply chain visibility and tracking. Unilever improved efficiency, cut down on waste, and adopted eco-friendly procedures across their whole supply chain by using digital tools.

Example 10: Domino's Pizza

Domino's Pizza created a digital road map to completely change the way pizza is ordered and delivered. They planned to invest money in things like chatbots, online ordering systems, and inventory monitors. Domino's increased customer satisfaction, simplified the ordering process, and enabled real-time order tracking by embracing digital technologies.

Example 11: Marriott International

To better serve guests and improve operations, Marriott International has adopted a digital road map. They spent money on convenient amenities like mobile check-in and check-out, keyless entrance, and individualised suggestions. Marriott was able to improve the guest experience by providing more individualised service and making it possible for guests to have more seamless interactions by utilising digital capabilities.

Example 12: Burberry

Burberry's digital roadmap prioritises developing an integrated and engaging multichannel experience for its customers. They used digital screens and augmented reality (AR) mirrors to incorporate technology into their flagship stores. Burberry improved the shopping experience by giving customers new, exciting opportunities to engage with the company's products by fusing the offline and online worlds.

Comparison and Analysis

As we compare the digital road maps of Amazon, Netflix, and Walmart, some common themes and best practices begin to emerge.

- Customer-centric approach

- Focus on innovation and continuous improvement

- Data-driven decision-making using

- Willingness to experiment and take risks

- They make use of Agile methodology

- Prioritize the use of technology to streamline their operations, with a particular emphasis on automation and artificial intelligence

- Prioritize collaboration and cross-functional teams

Key Takeaways

These common themes and best practices provide valuable insights for other organizations seeking to embark on their own digital transformation journeys. By adopting a customer-centric approach, embracing innovation and experimentation, prioritizing data-driven decision-making, and leveraging technology to streamline operations, companies can position themselves for success in a rapidly evolving digital landscape.

5.5 Good to know: Best lean and digital tools

Digital transformation can be a daunting task for many organizations, especially those with large and complex structures. In order to navigate the challenges that come with digitization, companies must leverage the right tools and strategies to ensure their success. Lean Digital tools are an essential component of this process, as they help organizations streamline their operations and reduce waste while improving efficiency and effectiveness. Lean tools can help organizations focus on their core business objectives and improve the quality of their products and services, ultimately leading to better customer satisfaction and increased revenue.

TOOL 1: LEAN CANVAS

The Lean Canvas is a visual tool that helps companies to define and validate their business models. It is a one-page document that outlines the key components of a business, such as customer segments, value proposition, channels, customer relationships, revenue streams, key resources, key activities, key partnerships, and cost structure. The Lean Canvas provides a framework for companies to quickly test and iterate on their business model, and to pivot if necessary.

In the context of digital transformations, the Lean Canvas can be used to define the digital strategy and business model of the company, and to align the different teams and stakeholders around a common vision.

Pros

- Provides a simple and visual way to communicate the business model and strategy of the company

- Allows for rapid iteration and testing of different business models and assumptions

- Helps to identify key risks and uncertainties early in the process

- Encourages cross-functional collaboration and alignment

Cons

- Can oversimplify complex business models and strategies
- May not be suitable for highly regulated industries or complex value chains
- Requires a high level of expertise to facilitate the process effectively

How to Use in Digital Lean Environment?

- Use in the ideation stage to test and refine business ideas

Case Study:

One example of a company that successfully used a Lean Canvas in their digital transformation is **Airbnb**. In the early days of the company, the founders used the Lean Canvas to rapidly test and iterate on different business models, such as providing breakfast and local tours. They were able to identify the key components of their business model, such as the importance of trust between hosts and guests, and the need for a simple and user-friendly platform. This allowed them to pivot their business model and focus on what really mattered to their customers, which ultimately led to their success.

TOOL 2: KANBAN

Kanban is a visual tool that is used to manage workflow and increase productivity in a Lean Digital environment. It is based on the principle of just-in-time production and involves the use of a board with columns that represent different stages of a process, with each task or project represented by a card or sticky note. Kanban boards can be physical or digital, and the system allows team members to easily see the status of each task or project in real-time.

Pros:

- Improves workflow and productivity by visualizing work progress
- Promotes collaboration and communication among team members
- Encourages continuous improvement by identifying bottlenecks and inefficiencies
- Provides flexibility in managing workloads and priorities
- Can be easily customized to fit the needs of different teams and projects

Cons:

- May require training for team members who are not familiar with the Kanban system
- May not be suitable for complex projects that require detailed project management tools

- May not be effective in teams that have a high level of uncertainty and variability in their workflow

How to Use in Digital Lean Environment?

- Use to visualize and optimize workflows
- Minimize bottlenecks and increase productivity in agile digital environments

Case Study:

One example of a company that successfully used Kanban in their digital transformation is **Zara**, the Spanish clothing retailer. Zara used Kanban boards to manage the workflow of their design and production teams, allowing them to quickly identify and address bottlenecks in the production process. By visualizing their workflow and improving communication among team members, Zara was able to increase the speed of their production process and maintain a competitive edge in the fashion industry.

TOOL 3: AGILE METHODOLOGY

Agile Methodology is a project management approach that emphasizes flexibility, collaboration, and incremental progress. It is often used in software development and other digital transformation projects because it allows for changes to be made throughout the process as feedback is received.

Pros:

- Improved project visibility and control
- Higher customer satisfaction due to continuous delivery and feedback
- Increased team collaboration and communication
- Faster time-to-market through shorter development cycles

Cons:

- May require more resources and time than traditional project management approaches
- May not be suitable for projects with fixed scope and deadlines
- Requires a high level of stakeholder engagement and buy-in

How to Use in Digital Lean Environment?

- Use to prioritize customer needs and iterate quickly
- Adapt to changing market trends and enhance team collaboration

Case Study:

Spotify is a great example of a company that has successfully implemented agile methodology in its digital transformation. By organizing its development teams into autonomous squads, Spotify was able to increase collaboration, flexibility, and speed of delivery. This allowed them to continuously improve their music streaming service and maintain their competitive edge in the industry.

TOOL 4: VALUE STREAM MAPPING

Value Stream Mapping is a lean tool used to visualize and analyze the flow of materials, information, and actions required to deliver a product or service to the customer. It can be used to identify areas of waste, bottlenecks, and inefficiencies in a process, and to develop a plan for improvement. In the context of digital transformations, Value Stream Mapping can be used to map out the end-to-end process of a digital product or service, from ideation to delivery, and to identify areas for improvement.

Pros:

- Provides a visual representation of the process, making it easier to identify areas of waste and inefficiency
- Helps to identify bottlenecks and areas where work is piling up
- Facilitates cross-functional collaboration and communication by providing a shared understanding of the process
- Can help to reduce lead times, increase efficiency, and improve customer satisfaction

Cons:

- Can be time-consuming and resource-intensive to create the map and analyze the data
- Requires input and buy-in from all stakeholders involved in the process
- May not be effective in identifying issues that are not visible in the current process or system
- Value Stream Mapping can be used in a variety of industries and processes, including software development, customer service, and supply chain management

How to Use in Digital Lean Environment?

- Use Value Stream Mapping to identify and eliminate non-value-added activities
- Use to Optimize processes and improve customer experience

Table 2: Best Lean & Digital Tools

Tool	Mean	Where to use	Pros	Cons	Environment
Lean Canvas	Strategic Planning	Start-ups, New Product Development	Simplifies Business Model Planning	Lack of Detailed Analysis	Innovation and Start-ups
Kanban	Visual Management	Project Management, Software Development	Increased Visibility and Efficiency	Limited in Handling Complex Processes	Agile Environment
Agile Methodology	Project Management	Software Development, Product Launch	Flexibility, Customer Collaboration	Requires strong team Collaboration	Dynamic Projects
Value Stream Mapping	Process Mapping	Manufacturing, Service Improvement	Identifies and eliminates waste	Time Consuming to create	Operational Excellence
Continuous Improvement	Problem Solving	All Areas of Business	Ongoing Efficiency gains	Resistance to change	Cultures of Continuous Improvement
Lean Six Sigma	Process Improvement	Manufacturing, Health Care, Finance	Data Driven Decision Making	Requires Skilled Personnel	Process Intensive Industries
Scrum	Agile Framework	Software, Development, Product Delivery	Iterative Development, Adaptive Planning	Dependency on Team Collaboration	Agile Environment
Design Thinking	Innovation	Product Design, Problem Solving	Human-Centric, Creative problem solving	May Lack concrete implementation plans	Creative and Design context
DevOps	IT Operations	Software Development, IT Operations	Accelerated Delivery, Collaboration	Initial Implementation Efforts	IT Environment
Lean Portfolio Management	Strategic Planning	Project Portfolio Management, Organisational Change	Aligns Strategy with Execution	Requires Cultural Transformation	Large Scale Organisations

5.5.1 15 Case Studies of Successful Use of Lean Digital Tools by Large Organisations

Many businesses in many fields have benefited from the efficiency gains, increased customer satisfaction, and overall success that have resulted from using Lean Digital solutions. To demonstrate the value of Lean Digital tools, we'll look at 15 case studies of companies that have effectively adopted them.

- **Toyota:** Toyota, an industry leader in lean manufacturing, has embraced the use of digital tools throughout the company's assembly lines. Manufacturing operations are optimised, waste is decreased, and productivity is increased by using real-time data analytics, digital Kanban systems, and robot automation.

- **Amazon:** Amazon uses numerous digital lean tools to improve its business and the shopping experience for its customers. In order to streamline inventory management, order processing, and shipping procedures, they use cutting-edge data analytics, machine learning algorithms, and robotic automation in their distribution centres.

- **Zara:** Zara, The world-famous clothing retailer, has adopted digital lean methods to revamp its supply chain. Reduced inventory costs and a flexible supply chain are the results of their use of real-time data analytics and digital communication systems for keeping tabs on stock, keeping tabs on consumer preferences, and reacting swiftly to market demands.

- **Siemens:** Siemens is using Lean Digital tools to enhance production. They use digital twins, Internet of Things (IoT) sensors, and predictive analytics to keep tabs on machinery, ensure regular upkeep, and cut down on unplanned downtime. The results have been better operational efficiency, lower expenses, and more productivity.

- **Starbucks:** Starbucks has used digital lean tools to improve the in-store experience for customers and boost overall business efficiency. In order to cut down on wait times and boost customer happiness, they use digital payment methods, data analytics, and personalised product offerings to streamline the ordering process.

- **GE Aviation:** GE Aviation has improved its maintenance and repair operations with the help of Lean Digital tools. Predictive analytics, Internet of Things (IoT)-enabled sensors, and machine learning algorithms are used to keep an eye on the engine, spot any problems, and plan for preventative upkeep. As a result, aircraft dependability, maintenance costs, and operational efficiency have all increased.

- **BMW:** BMW has optimised its manufacturing processes by incorporating Lean Digital tools. To track production line efficiency, pinpoint problems, and make changes, they use data analytics, robotic automation, and Internet of Things connectivity. Because of this, BMW has increased output, reduced cycle times, and enhanced product quality.

- **Delta Air Lines:** Delta Air Lines makes use of Lean Digital solutions to improve efficiency and service to passengers. Check-in procedures are streamlined, passengers are kept up-to-date in real time, and service is tailored to each individual through the use of mobile apps, self-service kiosks, and digital communication systems. Because of this, things are running more efficiently, there are fewer lines, and customers are happier than ever.

- **Intel:** Intel has embraced Lean Digital tools to improve production efficiency and push the company towards operational excellence. To boost yield rates, find flaws, and increase production efficiency, they use real-time data analytics, AI-driven quality control systems, and automation. As a result, product quality is up, expenses are down, and patronage is up.

- **Walmart:** The supply chain and retail operations at Walmart have been modernised with the use of Lean Digital tools. They use analytics, RFID, and a streamlined replenishment system to improve product availability, customer service, and the store's bottom line.

- **Johnson & Johnson:** Manufacturing and supply chain efficiency were both greatly enhanced by Johnson & Johnson's adoption of Lean Digital tools. To maximise stock, lessen lead times, and guarantee on-time product delivery, they employ real-time production monitoring, demand forecasting algorithms, and supply chain visibility technologies.

- **Ford:** To enhance operational efficiency and quality control, Ford has adopted Lean Digital technologies in its production processes. Improved product quality and less rework are the results of the use of digital sensors, Internet of Things connectivity, and real-time analytics to track the efficiency of production lines, identify problems, and take corrective action in real time.

- **Coke:** Coke improved its distribution and supply chain efficiency with the use of Lean Digital tools. To boost delivery productivity, cut down on transportation expenses, and eliminate shop stockouts, they use data analytics, route optimisation algorithms, and real-time tracking systems.

- **Lufthansa:** Lufthansa has improved its maintenance and repair operations with the use of Lean Digital tools. They use predictive maintenance algorithms, digital documentation systems, and augmented reality tools to boost the effectiveness of aviation maintenance, decrease unscheduled downtime, and increase the output of maintenance crews.

- **Tesco:** To better manage its stock and streamline its supply chain, retail giant Tesco has used Lean Digital tools. They optimise stock, cut down on waste, and boost supply chain efficiency through the use of data analytics, demand forecasting algorithms, and automated replenishment systems

Key Takeaways

While each tool has its unique strengths and weaknesses, there are common themes and best practices that successful organizations have employed when implementing these tools. These tools emphasize the importance of collaboration and communication, as well as the importance of flexibility and adaptability.

Successful organizations have found ways to measure and track progress using data and metrics. Whether it is tracking the number of tasks completed in Kanban or analyzing the impact of a Continuous Improvement initiative, data-driven decision making is crucial for understanding what is working and what needs improvement. To apply these themes and best practices to one's own organization, it is important to start by identifying the specific challenges and goals of the digital transformation.

Chapter Summary

The difficulties of digital transformation and technology's function as an enabler of processes are discussed in Chapter 5, "Focus 4: Technology is a Process Enabler Only: Why 90% of Digital Transformation Fails." Differentiating between digitization, digitalization, digital transformation, and Lean Digital is just one of the many issues covered in this chapter. It delves into the state of Industry 5.0, shows how other companies have implemented effective digital roadmaps, and features the most useful digital and lean resources.

- The chapter presents an overview of the difficulties encountered by organisations during digital lean projects, drawing attention to the nuances and roadblocks that can arise on the path to digital transformation.

- It makes it easier to understand the differences between terms like "digitization," "digitalization," "digital transformation," and "Lean Digital," all of which have important implications for business procedures and strategy.

- To determine if businesses are prepared to take advantage of emerging technologies and fully embrace the next stage of industrial transformation, this chapter analyses the preparedness of Industry 5.0.

- Example Digital Roadmaps That Have Been Successfully Implemented By Other Organisations This section provides examples of digital roadmaps that have been successfully implemented by other organisations in order to inspire and advise readers in their own digital transformation efforts.

- This chapter provides a high-level overview of the most useful lean and digital tools now accessible, illuminating for readers how these tools can be used to boost productivity, foster fruitful collaboration, and propel digital transformation efforts to fruition.

The goal of these considerations is to provide readers with the knowledge and skills they need to successfully traverse the digital landscape, including a thorough appreciation of the pitfalls associated with digital transformation.

Key Questions for Readers

1. What are the most significant challenges affecting digital lean projects? How can businesses deal with these issues and overcome roadblocks to digital transformation to achieve success?

2. The terms "digitization," "digitalization," "digital transformation," and "Lean Digital" all sound similar; what are the differences between them? How does each idea aid in the development of organisational procedures and plans?

3. Can we finally launch Industry 5.0? How can businesses best adopt Industry 5.0 and take advantage of upcoming technologies, and what kind of improvements and capacities will they need to do so?

4. Can you give me any case studies of organisations that have successfully used digital roadmaps? What lessons about methods, processes, and outcomes can be drawn from these cases to inform and motivate digital transformation initiatives?

5. Where can I get the most effective digital and lean resources? How might these resources improve digital transformation projects' productivity, teamwork, and ultimate success?

147

Part Six

Focus Five: Make Your own Sustainable Game Plan

One Team One Goal- Plan together to succeed together

"Building a visionary company requires one percent vision and 99 percent alignment."

~Jim Collins and Jerry Porras

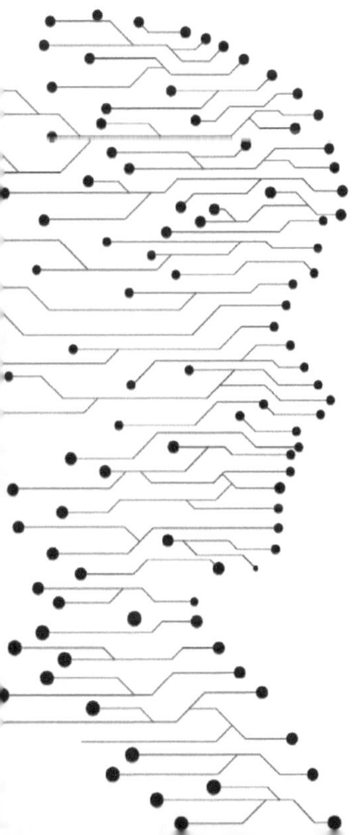

There were some businesses that consistently excelled despite the dynamic nature of digital transformation. In addition to being technologically savvy, these businesses had a firm grasp on lean principles. Let's learn more about them and figure out what made them so successful.

Get to know XYZ Corporation, an international powerhouse in the software business. XYZ Corporation saw the importance of adapting lean practises to the digital sphere, thus they made an effort to implement them. They started along the path of Lean Digital Transformation, bringing all of their new tech in line with lean practises.

Constantly placing the needs of their customers first was the first major factor in XYZ Corporation's success. They realised that in the digital age, consumers place an emphasis on individualised service and frictionless communication. In order to fuel their digital efforts, XYZ Company actively sought client feedback. Insight into customers' problems and wants led to novel approaches that provided real satisfaction.

In addition, XYZ Corporation encouraged its employees to always seek out new ways to develop and innovate. They fostered an environment where employees felt safe questioning assumptions and offering novel ideas. They used a kaizen approach to their digital processes, continuously looking for ways to improve efficiency and cut down on waste.

XYZ Company has adopted agile methods to aid their Lean Digital initiatives. They set up interdisciplinary groups to foster communication, cooperation, and rapid prototyping. Scrum and kanban, two examples of agile practises, helped them improve communication, shorten development cycles, and speed up the rollout of their digital solutions.

6.1.1 Listed below are 10 Leading Examples of Lean Digital Businesses

Manufacturing Industries:

- **General Electric (GE)**

Jeff Immelt, Leader of General Electric

Methodology: Using digital tools, analytics, and lean techniques to boost efficiency, quality, and innovation in the factory Strategic alliances with tech firms, a data-driven culture, and top-down support for digital transformation all play a role.

- **Siemens**

Joe Kaeser, Leader of Siemens

Methodology: Increasing productivity and creativity in the factory through the use of digital tools like robots, AI, and data analytics.

Critical to our success has been our dedication to funding R&D, investment in our digital infrastructure, and commitment to a culture of constant improvement.

- **Bosch**

Volkmar Denner, Leader of Bosch

Method: Using digital technologies and lean concepts to boost efficiency, automate more tasks, and enhance quality. Innovation, partnerships with new businesses, and a focus on the end user are crucial to the success of any product development process.

- **BMW**

Oliver Zipse, the leader

Method: Embedding digital technology into production, supply chain management, and the customer experience to boost output, efficiency, and individualization.

Research and development investing, a commitment to sustainability responsibility, and nimbleness in meeting customer needs are all desirable qualities.

Non-Manufacturing Industries:

- **Google**

Sundar Pichai, the leader

Methodology: Using digital tools, data analytics, and machine learning to fine-tune search algorithms, create revolutionary products, and personalise services for each individual user. Innovation, never-ending education, and a culture that encourages taking risks are emphasised.

- **Apple**

Tim Cook, the leader

Method: Using digital technologies, customer-centric design, and supply chain optimisation to create satisfied customers, excellent end results, and a devoted clientele. Investment in R&D, a memorable brand identity, and meticulous attention to design and user experience are all essential.

- **Amazon**

Leader: Jeff Bezos

Methodology: Streamlining supply chain processes, improving customer experiences, and driving innovation through the use of digital technology, data analytics, and lean principles. Customers come first, decisions are made based on data, new ideas are constantly developed, and efficiency is prioritised.

- **Airbnb**

Brian Chesky, Leader

Methodology: Using digital platforms, data analytics, and user-generated content to revolutionise the hotel sector, personalise guests' trips, and establish a reliable network. The scalability of the platform, user involvement, brand recognition, and user trust are all crucial elements.

- **Uber**

Dara Khosrowshahi, the leader

Method: Embracing digital infrastructures, analytics, and mobile devices to revolutionise transportation operations and provide superior service to passengers. Focus on driver and passenger safety, data-driven decision-making, flexible pricing structures, and a streamlined user experience.

- **Netflix**

Reed Hastings, the leader

The strategy involves disrupting the entertainment sector through the seamless integration of digital streaming technology, personalised content recommendations, and data analytics. Constant experimentation with new methods of delivering content, data-driven algorithms, user involvement, and an emphasis on original programming are all crucial to achieving this goal.

6.1.2 10 Lessons All Leaders can Learn from their Achievements

Successful Lean Digital businesses know that digital transformation is much more than just updating their technology. To achieve operational excellence, customer centricity, and sustained growth, they know they need to integrate digital capabilities with lean principles. Key features and lessons learned from their success include the following:

- Customer-Centric Mindset: Successful businesses place an emphasis on learning about and satisfying their customers' wants and requirements, and they do this through the use of consumer surveys, data analytics, and customised offerings.

- Agile and Adaptive Culture: They encourage staff to accept change and try out new ideas, creating an environment that is both flexible and innovative.

- Data-Driven Decision Making: They use data and analytics to improve decision-making, boost efficiencies in operations, and identify untapped market niches.

- Seamless Digital Experience: These businesses aim to provide a seamless digital experience for their customers by offering intuitive interfaces, personalised product suggestions, and easy, paperless financial transactions across all major digital channels.

- Lean Operations: These businesses follow the tenets of lean management in order to increase productivity at every stage of the value chain.

- Strategic Partnerships: To gain access to expertise, propel innovation, and grow operations, successful Lean Digital businesses form strategic alliances with technology suppliers, startups, and industry leaders.

- Investment in People: The company places a premium on training and retaining experts in fields like data analytics, AI, and UX design.

- Innovation: These businesses make innovation a top priority and foster an environment where employees are free to come up with new ideas, try things out, and learn from their mistakes.

- Risk Management: They take precautions against threats related to the digital transition, such as data breaches, privacy violations, and noncompliance with regulations.

- Leadership Commitment: Successful Lean Digital businesses include leaders who promote digital transformation, set an exemplary example, and foster an environment conducive to change.

Key Takeaways

Adopt a customer-first philosophy and use information to predict and fulfil their needs.

Create an environment where change is welcomed and creativity is celebrated.

invest in digital infrastructure and train employees to be proficient with digital tools.

Ensure that digital experiences are consistent across all points of contact with customers.

To improve productivity, efficiency, and effectiveness, adopt a lean mindset.

Seek out strategic alliances to gain access to technological expertise and propel innovation.

Foster an environment where people are always trying new things and learning.

Protect sensitive information and manage other hazards that come with digital change.

Show your dedication to the digital transition by setting an example.

Accept alteration and welcome novel approaches and tools.

Organisations that want to succeed in the digital age must undertake a Lean Digital Transformation journey. This section provides you with the tools you need to generate digital excellence and competitive advantage by outlining 10 critical steps to implement Lean Digital Transformation, complete with examples from the author's own experience.

- **Put Your Goals Into Action:** "Sparking Innovation in Digital Media" Create an inspiring digital vision that supports organisational goals. For instance, GE has a goal of joining the ranks of the world's top 10 software companies by implementing the principles of the industrial internet.

- **Analyse Where We Are Now** by "Showing the Way Forward." Evaluate all of your current procedures, infrastructure, and digital resources to find places for growth. Domino's Pizza is one company that updated its online ordering system to better serve its customers.

- **Make a Team That Works Across Departments:** "Unleashing Collaborative Forces" Create a multidisciplinary group representing different departments to encourage communication, cooperation, and shared responsibility for the transition. If you want to see how cross-departmental cooperation can propel digital change, look no further than Salesforce's Trailblazer programme.

- **Focus on Your Goals and Start** "Charting the Course for success." Establish clear, quantifiable goals to direct the change and ensure it advances the company's long-term objectives. The mission of Netflix to become the preeminent streaming platform in the world is an excellent example of well-defined transformational aims.

- **Create a Guide:** "Mapping the Digital Expedition".

- **Make a plan** that includes the initiatives, milestones, and dependencies in detail. The British Broadcasting Corporation (BBC) has a detailed plan to upgrade its digital content distribution infrastructure.

- **Invest in Your Staff's** Development and Training: "Equipping Digital Leaders"

- **Improve digital skills** and foster a mindset of lifelong learning by funding training and upskilling programmes. Adobe's Digital Academy programme provides employees with the tools they need to become proficient in digital media.

- **The importance** of "Nurturing Digital Mavericks" in fostering an environment favourable to innovation Incentivize and celebrate the development of novel digital approaches. The "20% time" policy at Google, in which employees are encouraged to concentrate on personal projects, is a prime example of the company's innovative culture.

- **Agile methods**: "Embracing Agile Velocity"

Use agile practises to drive iterative, collaborative development, which increases flexibility and shortens the time it takes to bring a product to market. Agile and the Spotify Model have been instrumental in streamlining Spotify's product development and delivery processes.

- **Use "Capturing the Digital Revolution" to take advantage of cutting-edge tech.**

Leverage AI, the Internet of Things (IoT), and data analytics to discover untapped prospects. The use of cutting-edge automation and artificial intelligence in Tesla's electric automobiles is illustrative of the transformative potential of modern technology.

- **"Exploring the Digital Seas" is a process of constant monitoring and optimisation.**

Keep an eye on KPIs, solicit feedback, and adjust your strategy as needed to achieve your goals. A good example is Amazon's focus on the consumer by using analytics data to provide specific suggestions.

6.3 Lean Digital Transformation Principles

Organisations now need to adopt lean concepts to drive effective digital transformations in order to keep up with the ever-changing digital landscape. Optimising processes, enhancing customer experiences, and achieving operational excellence are all possible when firms combine lean approaches with digital initiatives. This section delves into the five principles of Lean Digital transformation, providing a guide for businesses just starting out on their digital adventure.

- **"Customer-First Thinking: Sparking Change Through Focus on the Customer"**

Successful Lean Digital transformation requires companies to adopt a "customer-first mindset." The necessity of knowing one's customers' wants, needs, and problems is emphasised in this principle. Digital solutions that provide outstanding value and engaging experiences may be developed by businesses by collecting customer insights, utilising data analytics, and implementing user-centric design thinking. By putting the client first, you can guarantee that your digital initiatives will meet the needs of your target audience and even help you stand out from the competition online.

- **"Iterative Improvement is the Cornerstone of the Lean Digital Transformation Approach"**

Digital innovation is fueled by a culture of experimentation, feedback loops, and the willingness to change. Agile approaches allow businesses to quickly test, and iterate digital solutions in order to adapt to shifting market conditions and cutting-edge technological developments. Businesses may thrive in today's rapidly evolving digital landscape by embracing a culture of learning and innovation.

- **"Optimising Value Streams to Achieve Digital Excellence"**

Lean Digital transformation centres on value stream optimisation. This guiding principle seeks to minimise effort and maximise productivity by emphasising these goals. Bottlenecks, duplications, and inefficiencies in digital processes can be uncovered by mapping the full scope of such processes. By using value stream mapping and other lean technologies, businesses may streamline operations, shorten production cycles, and better satisfy consumers. By optimising the value stream, we can guarantee that our digital projects will help us achieve our business goals and give us a competitive edge that will last.

- **"Collaborative Development: Fostering a Culture of Cross-Functional Collaboration"**

The key to a successful Lean Digital transition is a culture of collaborative empowerment. The goal of this guiding concept is to encourage cooperation between departments. Organisations can benefit from the intelligence, creativity, and competence of the group by assembling people from many different walks of life. When employees are able to work together, they are better able to share knowledge, spark new ideas, and speed up the adoption of digital solutions. Organisations may better deal with digital issues and generate transformational outcomes by encouraging team members to work together effectively.

- **"Insight-Driven, Data-Driven Decision Making for Digital Success"**

One of the cornerstones of Lean Digital transformation is the use of data to inform decisions. In order to make use of the insights they uncover, businesses need to employ data analytics, AI, and machine learning. With the right data at their disposal, businesses can streamline operations, increase productivity, and propel their digital transformation. Understanding client behaviour, increasing operational efficiency, and fostering innovation in the digital sphere are all emphasised by this guiding principle.

Key Takeaways

> Organisations may succeed in the digital age if they adopt the five principles of Lean Digital transformation: focus on the customer, work in small, continuous increments, optimise the value stream, empower employees to work together, and make decisions based on data. The concepts laid out here offer a road map to digital mastery, customer satisfaction, and long-term success in the information age.

6.4 The 8 Different Kinds of Digital Waste in Lean Management

Although Lean thinking was developed in the context of manufacturing, it is just as applicable to the digital world. Organisations may optimise their digital operations by learning to recognise the eight different forms of Lean Digital waste. This section will provide an in-depth examination of each type of waste, illustrated with concrete instances.

Overproduction:

When it comes to digital assets like reports, papers, and data, overproduction occurs when more are created or generated than are required. Information overload, diminished focus, and lost resources are all possible outcomes of this sort of waste. Daily report production that exceeds needs and is rarely evaluated is a prime example of overproduction.

Waiting:

Digital processes or people lose time waiting when they sit inactive because of things like dependencies or a lack of coordination. Unproductive waiting occurs, for example, when a team member awaits authorization or comments. Waiting waste can also result from inefficient email procedures, which cause activities to be delayed due to slow response times.

Transportation:

Wasteful movement or transfer of digital assets, such as files or data, between systems or people is known as transportation waste in Lean Digital Transformation. Inefficient practises include copying and pasting information from one programme to another instead of integrating the necessary systems for seamless data flow.

Overprocessing:

Digital procedures that are performed multiple times without improving the final product are examples of overprocessing. Some examples of overprocessing waste include redundant data cleansing and validation procedures that add no value to the data.

Inventory:

The term "inventory waste" is used to describe the practise of collecting unnecessary quantities of digital assets such as unneeded files, redundant code, or obsolete data. This clutter can take up valuable disc space, slow down operations, and add layers of complexity to computerised tasks. Stock waste can be exacerbated by practises like retaining numerous copies of the same document or maintaining unnecessary backup files.

Motion:

During the execution of a process, motion waste occurs when there is an unneeded transfer of control from one point to another. In the digital world, this may involve a lot of mouse work, scrolling, or figuring out complicated interfaces. A software interface that is difficult to navigate and requires several clicks to accomplish a single goal is an example of motion waste.

Defects:

Errors, omissions, or faults in digital processes or outputs are collectively referred to as "defect waste." Time and energy are wasted on correcting mistakes, fixing bugs, and doing rework. Software with flaws that need to be debugged or patched before they will work properly is an example of defect waste.

Underutilization of Talent:

Talent underutilization occurs when people's knowledge, abilities, and experience are not used to their full potential. In the digital world, this waste can occur when employees are either not given enough training or are given assignments that are outside their skill sets. It's a major barrier to efficiency and new ideas.

6.4.1 Here are Eight Typical Instances of Digital Waste that Businesses Face

- **Overproduction:**

Company: XYZ Corporation

Waste: Creating an abundance of reports every day that no one reads and uses is a waste of time and resources.

Elimination: Reduced the number of superfluous reports and their frequency through the use of automated reporting systems that generate reports on demand.

Effects: The result was a reduction in the amount of information staff had to process and more time spent on things that directly provided value to the business.

- **Waiting:**

Company: ABC Inc.

Waste: Time wasted while awaiting code modifications to be approved by numerous parties.

Elimination: To get rid of it, we implemented an automatic approval system with well-defined notice and escalation points.

Effects: shorter development cycles, faster code reviews, and less developer downtime.

- **Transportation:**

Company: XYZ Corporation

Waste: reentering customers' information into multiple order processing databases by hand.

Elimination: To get rid of the problem, a unified customer relationship management (CRM) and order management system was implemented.

Effects: The result is less time spent processing orders and happier customers because human error has been reduced or eliminated.

- **Overprocessing:**

Company: ABC Inc.

Waste: During data analysis, wasting time manually validating and cleaning the data many times.

Elimination: Through the use of data analytics technologies for automating the validation and cleaning of data.

Effects: Analysis activities are more efficient, data processing times are shorter, and data quality is higher.

- **Inventory:**

Company: XYZ Corporation

Waste: Having several copies of the same file that are no longer relevant is a waste of time and space.

Elimination: Set up document version control protocols and implement a centralised document management system.

Effects: The results are less need for physical space to store data, easier access to previously stored data, and streamlined teamwork.

- **Motion:**

Company: ABC Inc.

Waste: The enterprise software makes it take too long to get from one place to another.

Elimination: To get rid of it, we gave the software a new user interface that is both user-friendly and efficient.

Effects: The result is faster task completion, less user irritation, and higher levels of adoption.

- **Defects:**

Company: XYZ Corporation

Waste: Iterative cycles of fixing software flaws

Elimination: To get rid of it, we used rigorous automated testing and code reviews.

Effects: Defects in software were reduced, quality was increased, and debugging time was cut in half.

- **Underutilization of Talent:**

Company: ABC Inc.

Waste: Putting employees to work that doesn't make use of their abilities.

Elimination: In order to get rid of them, we did some skill assessments and reorganised the departments accordingly.

Effects: The result was employees who were more fulfilled and an environment where everyone felt encouraged to keep learning.

Table 3: *20 Examples of digital wastes in businesses*

Waste Type	Company Name	Waste Description	Elimination Strategy	Impact
Overproduction	XYZ Corporation	Generating excessive daily reports that are rarely reviewed.	Implemented automated reporting tools for customized reports.	Reduced wasted time and effort, improved focus on value-added tasks.
Waiting	ABC Inc.	Delays in receiving feedback on code changes.	Implemented automated code review and approval system.	Reduced idle time, faster feedback loops, and accelerated development.
Transportation	XYZ Logistics	Manually transferring shipment data between systems.	Integrated customer management and transportation systems.	Reduced errors, improved data accuracy, and faster order fulfillment.
Overprocessing	ABC Manufacturing	Conducting redundant quality checks at multiple stages.	Implemented statistical process control and focused inspections.	Reduced inspection time, minimized production delays, and improved product quality.
Inventory	XYZ Retail	Stockpiling excess inventory of slow-moving products.	Implemented demand-driven inventory management system.	Reduced storage costs, minimized obsolescence, and improved cash flow.
Motion	ABC Technology	Excessive clicks and navigation in software applications.	Redesigned user interface to simplify workflows.	Improved productivity, reduced user frustration, and faster task completion.
Defects	XYZ Software Solutions	Fixing software bugs discovered during testing.	Implemented automated testing frameworks and code reviews.	Improved software quality, faster release cycles, and

Waste Type	Company Name	Waste Description	Elimination Strategy	Impact
				higher customer satisfaction.
Underutilization of Talent	ABC Consulting	Assigning highly skilled consultants to routine tasks.	Delegated tasks and implemented automation.	Improved consultant satisfaction, higher-quality deliverables, and increased revenue.
Waiting	XYZ Tech Solutions	Delays in receiving customer approvals for project milestones.	Implemented a streamlined approval process with clear timelines.	Reduced project delays, improved coordination, and faster project completion.
Transportation	ABC Logistics	Physically moving paper-based documents between departments.	Implemented a digital document management system.	Reduced manual handling, improved document traceability, and streamlined processes.
Overprocessing	XYZ Manufacturing	Excessive data entry and validation in multiple systems.	Integrated systems and implemented data synchronization.	Reduced manual effort, improved data accuracy, and eliminated redundant tasks.
Defects	ABC Software Company	Frequent software bugs causing system crashes.	Implemented automated error monitoring and bug tracking.	Reduced system downtime, improved stability, and increased customer satisfaction.

Waste Type	Company Name	Waste Description	Elimination Strategy	Impact
Inventory	XYZ E-commerce	Excess stock of low-demand items due to inaccurate forecasting.	Implemented data-driven demand forecasting algorithms.	Reduced inventory holding costs, minimized waste, and improved profitability.
Waiting	ABC Telecom	Delays in customer support response times.	Implemented a ticketing system with service level agreements.	Reduced customer wait times, improved satisfaction, and increased customer loyalty.
Motion	XYZ Financial Services	Multiple approvals and handoffs in loan application process.	Redesigned the process to reduce unnecessary steps and handoffs.	Streamlined loan processing, reduced cycle time, and improved customer experience.
Overproduction	ABC Media Company	Generating excessive content with low viewership.	Implemented data analytics to identify high-demand content.	Reduced content creation costs, improved viewership, and increased engagement.
Underutilization of Talent	XYZ Consulting	Skilled consultants performing administrative tasks.	Introduced task automation and streamlined workflows.	Increased consultant productivity, improved client satisfaction, and reduced costs.
Transportation	ABC Manufacturing	Moving physical prototypes between design and testing teams.	Implemented digital collaboration tools and virtual testing.	Reduced prototype transportation time, improved collaboration, and accelerated product development.

Waste Type	Company Name	Waste Description	Elimination Strategy	Impact
Overprocessing	XYZ Healthcare	Duplication of medical tests and procedures across departments.	Implemented centralized patient data system for access by all departments.	Eliminated redundant tests, reduced patient waiting time, and improved healthcare efficiency.
Defects	ABC Software Solutions	Frequent software errors due to manual code deployments.	Implemented automated deployment pipelines and version control.	Reduced deployment errors, improved software stability, and enhanced customer experience.

Key Takeaways

Overproduction: Don't give out too much knowledge; instead, focus on what's useful.

Waiting Time: To be efficient, keep digital processes as quick as possible.

Transportation: Simplify the flow of digital data to stop sending data that doesn't need to be sent.

Processing Waste: Get rid of digital process steps that aren't needed.

Inventory: Get rid of unnecessary data storage by putting important information first.

Motion Waste: Make the user experience better so that it's easy to navigate.

Defects: To avoid mistakes, keep digital tools up to date and in good shape.

Underutilised Talent: Make sure that teams have the skills and tools they need to make the most of digital resources.

6.5 CEOs & Other Leaders Action Plan

There are several different roles played during Lean Digital Transformation by functions like HR, Lean, Finance, Digital and so on.

Table 4: Functions Roles During Transformation

Function	Roles	Challenges	Actions
HR	- Drive cultural change	- Resistance to change	- Develop and communicate a change management plan
	- Foster employee engagement	- Skill gaps and training needs	- Provide training and development programs
	- Align workforce with transformation goals	- Retention of key talent	- Redefine job roles and responsibilities
Lean	- Lead Lean initiatives	- Overcoming resistance to Lean practices	- Educate and train employees on Lean principles
	- Identify process improvement opportunities	- Sustaining Lean efforts over time	- Implement Lean tools and methodologies
Finance	- Ensure financial viability of transformation	- Allocating resources for transformation	- Conduct cost-benefit analysis
	- Monitor and report financial performance	- Budget constraints	- Implement financial controls and metrics
Digital	- Develop digital strategy and roadmap	- Legacy system integration	- Implement digital technologies and solutions
	- Enable digital capabilities across the organization	- Data privacy and security	- Foster digital literacy and training
Supply Chain	- Streamline supply chain processes	- Supplier management	- Implement supply chain automation

Function	Roles	Challenges	Actions
	- Improve inventory management	- Demand forecasting and planning	- Collaborate with suppliers for process efficiency
Sales	- Align sales strategies with transformation goals	- Changing customer expectations	- Implement customer-centric sales approach
	- Develop digital sales channels	- Salesforce adoption and training	- Utilize data analytics for sales forecasting
Quality	- Ensure product/service quality	- Standardizing quality across processes	- Implement quality management systems
	- Continuous improvement of quality processes	- Root cause analysis and problem-solving	- Conduct quality audits and performance reviews
Safety	- Promote a culture of safety	- Identifying and mitigating safety risks	- Implement safety protocols and training
	- Ensure compliance with safety regulations	- Employee engagement in safety initiatives	- Conduct safety inspections and evaluations
Procurement	- Optimize procurement processes	- Supplier selection and management	- Implement strategic sourcing and vendor management
	- Cost reduction through efficient procurement	- Negotiating contracts and terms	- Conduct supplier performance evaluations
Legal	- Ensure legal compliance	- Managing legal risks and challenges	- Review and update legal policies and procedures
	- Provide legal support for transformation	- Contract management and negotiation	- Identify and mitigate legal risks
Commercial	- Drive customer-centric approach	- Market analysis and competition	- Develop customer loyalty programs

Function	Roles	Challenges	Actions
	- Identify new business opportunities	- Pricing and contract negotiations	- Foster collaboration with marketing and sales
IT/IS	- Enable digital infrastructure and systems	- Legacy system integration and migration	- Implement IT infrastructure and systems
	- Ensure data privacy and security	- System downtime and reliability	- Provide IT support and training

6.5.1 Key Leaders Action Plan

This table presents several roles played by CEOs, CFOs & by many other people & challenges faced by them. It presents what are the actions that can be taken during Lean Digital Transformation.

Table 5: Roles Played by Leaders During Transformation

Leader	Major Roles	Challenges	Actions	Duration for Actions
CEO	- Provide strategic direction	- Leading change	- Set vision and goals	Throughout the transformation process
	- Drive cultural transformation	- Overcoming resistance	- Communicate the importance of Lean Digital Transformation	Throughout the transformation process
CFO	- Financial planning and allocation	- Allocating budget for transformation initiatives	- Conduct cost-benefit analysis	As required for each initiative
	- Monitor financial performance	- Ensuring cost control	- Evaluate and prioritize investments	Ongoing throughout the transformation process
CIO	- IT strategy and governance	- Legacy system integration	- Develop and execute digital roadmap	Throughout the transformation process

Leader	Major Roles	Challenges	Actions	Duration for Actions
	- Enable digital capabilities	- Data privacy and security	- Implement digital technologies and platforms	Throughout the transformation process
CTO	- Technology strategy and innovation	- Legacy system modernization	- Drive adoption of emerging technologies	Throughout the transformation process
	- Architecture and infrastructure planning	- Ensuring system scalability and reliability	- Evaluate and select technology vendors	Ongoing throughout the transformation process
COO	- Operational process optimization	- Overcoming resistance to change	- Implement Lean practices and process improvements	Throughout the transformation process
	- Enhance operational efficiency	- Standardizing and streamlining processes	- Monitor and measure operational performance	Ongoing throughout the transformation process
CHRO	- Talent management and development	- Skill gaps and training needs	- Implement change management initiatives	Throughout the transformation process
	- Foster employee engagement	- Retention of key talent	- Provide training and development programs	Ongoing throughout the transformation process
CSCO	- Supply chain optimization	- Supplier management	- Implement supply chain automation	Throughout the transformation process
	- Demand forecasting and planning	- Ensuring logistics and delivery efficiency	- Collaborate with suppliers for process efficiency	Ongoing throughout the transformation process
VP/ Director/ Manager	- Department-specific leadership roles	- Resistance to change within teams	- Communicate transformation	Throughout the transformation process

Leader	Major Roles	Challenges	Actions	Duration for Actions
			goals and expectations	
	- Drive process improvement initiatives	- Ensuring team alignment and collaboration	- Facilitate training and upskilling	Ongoing throughout the transformation process
All Others	- Execute transformation initiatives	- Adapting to new processes and tools	- Embrace change and actively participate	Ongoing throughout the transformation process

Key Takeaways

CEOs should present an appealing vision that fits with the values and goals of the organisation. Leaders need to quickly make decisions based on good information and a balance of risk and chance. Clear and regular communication builds trust and supports teamwork within an organisation.

Leaders should be open to change and work to make their organisations flexible and quick to react. Put the team's growth and development first to make sure there are plenty of qualified leaders in the future. Promote a culture of innovation where taking measured risks is seen as a way to keep getting better. Adhere to moral standards and social responsibility, which will help the economy grow in a way that benefits everyone.

6.6 Ten Guidelines For Implementing Lean Digital Transformation

Organisations can set themselves up for success when they follow some basic guidelines before embarking on the Lean Digital Transformation journey. Five guidelines that successful firms have followed will be discussed, along with real-world examples, and ten rules for implementing a successful Lean Digital Transformation will be provided in this section.

The 5 Rules of Prosperous Businesses

1. Leadership Dedication: Leaders are Essential to Progress Toyota, for instance, is a well-known firm that adheres to Lean principles, and they made sure that their senior executives were actively engaged in the transition.

2. Employee Empowerment: Involving and energising staff members is essential. Spotify, a digital music streaming company, has adopted Lean concepts and encouraged employee innovation through risk-taking and autonomy. As a result, the **company is now flexible and attentive to its clients' needs.**

3. Customer-Centric Approach: Amazon's customer-centric approach is at the forefront of its Lean Digital Transformation initiatives. Their digital platforms are constantly updated based on client feedback and data, making for a smooth and individualised experience.

4. Data-Driven Decision Making: Using data as the primary factor in making decisions has proven to be crucial for Netflix's success in its digital transformation efforts. Viewer data and preferences are analysed to generate customised suggestions, better content, and higher levels of user happiness.

5. Continuous Learning and Adaptation: As part of its digital transformation, GE (General Electric) adopted the Lean methodology, which emphasises continuous learning and adaptation. They adopted a mindset of constant improvement and change, encouraging a spirit of experimentation and innovation that ultimately boosted productivity and expansion.

Successful Lean Digital Transformation Deployment: 10 Rules/Guidelines for Executives

1. To get everyone on the same page, you should first clearly describe the initiative's goals and outcomes.

2. Create a thorough plan, including the transformational road map, key milestones, and resource allocation.

3. Examine current methods, tools, and digital capacities to spot problem areas.

4. Involve and Educate Employees at all levels and provide them with the training and tools they need to better grasp the ideas behind Lean and Digital Transformation.

5. Sequence efforts carefully to maximise effectiveness and prioritise those with the greatest potential payoff.

6. Conquer silos and promote cross-departmental cooperation to propel an all-encompassing change initiative.

7. The seventh step is to put money into digital capabilities by purchasing and implementing the software, hardware, and networks that will be used to achieve the transformation goals.

8. In order to keep track of your progress towards your objectives, you should define certain key performance indicators (KPIs) and assess them on a regular basis.

9. Create an environment where employees feel empowered to point out and improve upon any inefficiencies they encounter in the workplace.

10. Recognise and celebrate successes to keep staff motivated and momentum high throughout the transition process.

Key Takeaways

Finally, a culture of continuous learning, data-driven decision-making, a focus on the customer, and leadership support are all necessary for a successful Lean Digital Transformation. Organisations can confidently navigate their transformation journeys and achieve sustained success in the digital world by adhering to these rules and using real examples.

Chapter Summary

- Companies that have found success by adopting Lean Digital concepts are examined in this chapter to learn more about their strategy, practises, and organisational culture.

- In "10 Steps for Deploying Lean Digital Transformation," the author walks the reader through the steps necessary to implement Lean Digital transformation so that they may create a detailed plan and put it into action.

- This chapter focuses on the underlying principles of Lean Digital transformation and how they should be used to direct decision-making, process improvement, and organisational change.

- Learn how to recognise and eliminate inefficiencies, bottlenecks, and non-value-added tasks in your digital processes by familiarising yourself with Lean management's eight categories of digital waste.

- Key Leaders' Roles and Responsibilities During the Lean Digital Transformation This chapter provides an action plan for key leaders, such as CEOs, CFOs, CIOs, CTOs, COOs, and CHROs, outlining their specific roles and responsibilities during the transformation and providing guidance on how they can effectively drive the journey.

- To help readers overcome obstacles, include all relevant parties, and provide long-lasting outcomes, this article presents ten criteria for achieving Lean Digital transformation.

In sum, this chapter equips readers with the tools they need to create a long-term strategy for implementing Lean Digital transformation. It equips its readers with the knowledge and tools they need to successfully navigate their own transformation journeys through an examination of successful companies, the following of deployment steps, an understanding of Lean principles, the identification of digital waste, the creation of an action plan for leaders, and the implementation of guidelines.

- How do leading Lean Digital organisations function? What methods, routines, and cultural norms have helped them succeed?

- How do you go about implementing the 10 steps of Lean Digital transformation? What strategies may businesses employ to put these transformational stages into action?

- To what extent does Lean Digital Transformation adhere to what guiding principles? How can these ideas guide the transformation of an organisation as a whole?

- In the context of Lean management, what are the eight forms of digital waste? How can businesses find and eliminate these inefficiencies in their digital operations to maximise productivity?

- When undergoing a Lean Digital transformation, what course of action should CEOs and other top leaders take? How can these leaders most efficiently steer the transformation course and involve key players?

- If you were to conduct a Lean Digital transformation, what ten rules would you follow? How can businesses effectively implement these principles to secure stakeholder buy-in and long-term success?

Appendix

Don't Miss - Assessments For Leaders

The purpose of this survey is to evaluate your skills as a Lean Digital Leader and their impact on the organisation's ability to drive and implement a digital transformation. Respond to the following questions honestly, using a scale from 1 to 5, with 1 meaning "not at all" and 5 meaning "very high."

1. How well do you grasp the digital implementation of Lean principles?

• 1 2 3 4 5

2. To what extent do Lean Digital Transformation efforts support the overarching goals of the company?

1 2 3 4 5

3. How well do you explain Lean Digital Transformation's goals and advantages to your staff and other stakeholders?

• 1 2 3 4 5

4. How do you encourage and facilitate employee involvement in Lean Digital Transformation initiatives?

• 1 2 3 4 5

5. How well do you manage opposition to change and lead others through the Lean Digital Transformation process?

• 1 2 3 4 5

6. How do you optimise and streamline processes using digital technologies?

1 2 3 4 5

7.   How well do you recognise and rank internal opportunities for digital innovation and disruption?

• 1 2 3 4 5

8.   How well do you make decisions based on data, and how well do you use analytics for continuous improvement?

• 1 2 3 4 5

9.   How well do you encourage cooperation between different departments in your Lean Digital Transformation projects?

• 1 2 3 4 5

10. How well versed are you in the methods of digital risk management and governance?

• 1 2 3 4 5

11. How well do you monitor the development and results of your Lean Digital Transformation projects?

• 1 2 3 4 5

12. How successfully do you promote an environment where people are always trying new things and improving their methods?

• 1 2 3 4 5

13. How willing are you to invest in and provide resources for Lean Digital Transformation?

• 1 2 3 4 5

14. How open are you to leveraging digital ecosystems outside of your organisation for the sake of cooperation and growth?

• 1 2 3 4 5

15. How dedicated are you to learning and growing, especially in regards to Lean and Digital Transformation's cutting-edge trends and technologies?

• 1 2 3 4 5

Based on your answers, judge how capable you are as a Lean Digital Leader. Figure out what you're good at and what needs work. Keep in mind that, as a leader, you play a crucial role in ensuring the smooth rollout of Lean Digital Transformation.

Conclusion

In conclusion, this book advocates for a Lean Digital Transformation that places people at the forefront, recognizing that success in the VUCA world requires a holistic and adaptive approach. By prioritizing a people-centric culture, fostering agile leadership, empowering teams, and embracing continuous learning, organizations can navigate the challenges of the digital era with resilience and innovation.

Leaders must acknowledge that technology is a means to an end, and the true driver of transformation lies in the collective efforts and capabilities of individuals. By aligning with Lean principles and addressing the human aspects of change, organizations can not only survive but thrive in the face of uncertainty. This book serves as a guide for leaders who seek to lead their teams through the complexities of the digital age, focusing on the core element that ensures sustainable success – the people.

In What Ways Can The Status Quo Be Challenged?

Lean Digital leaders can challenge things in these ten different ways:

1. Promote an environment where people are always thinking of new ways to improve things.
2. Take advantage of new technology and investigate how it might be used to improve current procedures.
3. Encourage teamwork across departments and eliminate silos.
4. Question established beliefs and look for alternate viewpoints.
5. Encourage staff to try out new things and take calculated risks.
6. Be receptive to and responsive to input from customers.
7. Be adaptable and set an example.
8. Put money into the growth of your staff and offer them technological education.
9. Make it okay to challenge the status quo by fostering an atmosphere of open inquiry.
10. Recognise and reward those who think outside the box and who successfully implement change.

References

CHAPTER 1:

1. https://www2.deloitte.com/us/en/insights/focus/industry-4-0/lean-digital-manufacturing-transformation.html

2. https://www.mckinsey.com/business-functions/mckinsey-digital/our-insights/the-five-trademarks-of-agility

3. McKinsey & Company. (2018). Why digital transformations fail. Retrieved from https://www.mckinsey.com/business-functions/digital-mckinsey/our-insights/why-digital-transformations-fail

4. Harvard Business Review. (2019). Why so many high-profile digital transformations fail. Retrieved from https://hbr.org/2019/07/why-so-many-high-profile-digital-transformations-fail

5. McKinsey & Company. (2017). Breaking away: The secrets to scaling analytics. Retrieved from https://www.mckinsey.com/business-functions/mckinsey-digital/our-insights/breaking-away-the-secrets-to-scaling-analytics

6. MIT Sloan Management Review. (2020). The CIO's role in digital transformation. Retrieved from https://sloanreview.mit.edu/article/the-cios-role-in-digital-transformation

7. B. Flyvbjerg, N. Bruzelius, and W. Rothengatter, Megaprojects and Risk: An Anatomy of Ambition (Cambridge University Press, 2003)

8. L. S. Sproull and S. Kiesler, Connections: New Ways of Working in the Networked Organization (MIT Press, 1991)

9. R. Adler and M. Borys, "Two Types of Bureaucracy: Enabling and Coercive," Administrative Science Quarterly, vol. 41, no. 1, pp. 61-89, 1996.

10. Ries, E. (2011). The Lean Startup: How Today's Entrepreneurs Use Continuous Innovation to Create Radically Successful Businesses. Crown Business.

11. McKinsey & Company. (2019). Lean Management in the Digital Age. Retrieved from https://www.mckinsey.com/business-functions/operations/our-insights/lean-management-in-the-digital-age

12. Reddy, P. (2019). Applying Lean Principles in Digital Transformation. GE Digital. Retrieved from https://www.ge.com/digital/blog/applying-lean-principles-digital-transformation

13. Poppendieck, M., & Poppendieck, T. (2003). Lean software development: An agile toolkit. Addison-Wesley Professional.

14. Shook, J. (2003). Lean transformations: Lessons from the front lines. Lean Enterprise Institute.

15. Radnor, Z., & O'Brien, J. (2007). Lean in public services: Panacea or paradox? Public Money & Management, 27(3), 179-184.

16. Womack, J. P., Jones, D. T., & Roos, D. (1990). The machine that changed the world: The story of lean production. Free Press.

17. Davenport, T. H. (2018). The AI advantage: How to put the artificial intelligence revolution to work. MIT Press.

18. Kagermann, H., et al. (2013). IT-driven business models: Global case studies in transformation. Wiley.

19. Womack, J. P., Jones, D. T., & Roos, D. (2007). The machine that changed the world: The story of lean production—Toyota's secret weapon in the global car wars that is revolutionizing world industry. Simon and Schuster.

20. McAfee, A., & Brynjolfsson, E. (2017). Machine, platform, crowd: Harnessing our digital future. W. W. Norton & Company.

21. Kotter, J. P. (2012). Leading change. Harvard Business Review Press.

22. Sutherland, J. (2014). Scrum: The art of doing twice the work in half the time. Crown Business.

23. LaValle, S., et al. (2011). Big data, analytics and the path from insights to value. MIT Sloan Management Review.

24. Duhigg, C. (2016). Smarter faster better: The secrets of being productive in life and business. Random House.

CHAPTER 2:

1. Ulwick, A. W. (2005). What customers want: Using outcome-driven innovation to create breakthrough products and services. Harvard Business Press.

2. Rigby, D. K., Reichheld, F. F., & Schefter, P. (2002). Avoid the four perils of CRM. Harvard Business Review, 80(2), 101-109.

3. Parasuraman, A., Zeithaml, V. A., & Berry, L. L. (1985). A conceptual model of service quality and its implications for future research. Journal of Marketing, 49(4), 41-50.

4. Gompers, P. A., & Lerner, J. (1998). What drives venture capital fundraising? Brookings Papers on Economic Activity, 1998(2), 149-205.

5. Ayotte, K. M., & Helland, E. (2002). Venture capital and the valuation of start-up firms. The Journal of Finance, 57(6), 2495-2528.

6. Lockett, A., & Wright, M. (2001). The syndication of private equity: Evidence from the UK. Venture Capital: An International Journal of Entrepreneurial Finance, 3(3), 213-237.

7. McAfee, A., Brynjolfsson, E., Davenport, T. H., Patil, D. J., & Barton, D. (2012). Big data: The management revolution. Harvard Business Review, 90(10), 60-68.

8. Ross, J. W., Beath, C. M., & Goodhue, D. L. (2013). Develop long-term competitiveness through IT assets and capabilities. MIS Quarterly, 37(4), 1189-1210.

9. Westerman, G., Bonnet, D., & McAfee, A. (2014). Leading digital: Turning technology into business transformation. Harvard Business Review Press.

10. Gill, J., Johnson, P., & Whittle, S. (2017). Research methods for managers. Sage Publications.

11. McAllister, D. J. (1995). Affect- and cognition-based trust as foundations for interpersonal cooperation in organizations. Academy of Management Journal, 38(1), 24-59.

12. Kiron, D., Kruschwitz, N., Reeves, M., Goh, G., & van der Heyden, L. (2017). The jobs that artificial intelligence will create. MIT Sloan Management Review, 58(4), 14-17.

13. Purcell, J., Kinnie, N., Hutchinson, S., Rayton, B., & Swart, J. (2003). Understanding the people and performance link: Unlocking the black box. Research Report RR392. Institute for Employment Studies.

14. Kotter, J. P. (1996). Leading change. Harvard Business Review Press.

15. Nambisan, S., & Baron, R. A. (2009). Virtual customer environments: Testing a model of voluntary participation in value co-creation activities. Journal of Product Innovation Management, 26(4), 388-406.

16. Ries, E. (2011). The Lean Startup: How Today's Entrepreneurs Use Continuous Innovation to Create Radically Successful Businesses. Crown Business.

17. Westerman, G., Bonnet, D., & McAfee, A. (2014). Digital Transformation: A Roadmap for Billion-Dollar Organizations. Harvard Business Review.

18. Osterwalder, A., & Pigneur, Y. (2010). Business Model Generation: A Handbook for Visionaries, Game Changers, and Challengers. Wiley.

19. Lean Digital: The Rise of Human-Centered Digital Design" by Joanne Molesky, Jed R. Cawthorne, and Mark J. Price

20. Sánchez, J. A. (2017). Lean Digital Transformation: A Step-by-Step Guide to Building Lean Digital Capabilities. Springer.

21. Ragowsky, A., & Haddad, L. (2018). Lean Digital transformation: A new paradigm for delivering business transformation in the digital age. International Journal of Information Management, 39, 80-85.

22. Smith, J. A. (2021). The Lean Mindset: How to Transform Your Business with Lean Principles. Wiley.

23. Lean Customer Development: Building Products Your Customers Will Buy" by Cindy Alvarez

24. Lee, S., & Kim, S. (2019). The impact of digital technology on customer experience: a literature review. Journal of Service Management, 30(1), 37-57.

25. Hinterhuber, A., & Liozu, S. M. (2019). Lean Digital transformation: an overview. Journal of Revenue and Pricing Management, 18(4), 261-266.

26. Kim, S., Lee, S., & Kim, Y. (2020). The effect of Lean Digital transformation on customer experience in the hospitality industry. Journal of Hospitality and Tourism Technology, 11(1), 131-145.

27. Andriole, S. J. (2019). Lean Digital: The Rise of Continuous Improvement in the Digital Age. Taylor & Francis.

28. The Lean Startup: How Today's Entrepreneurs Use Continuous Innovation to Create Radically Successful Businesses" by Eric Ries

29. Furst, L., & Whipple, J. (2016). Lean Digital: leveraging the power of lean principles to transform digital customer engagement. Routledge.

30. Morgan, J., & Liker, J. K. (2021). The Toyota product development system: integrating people, processes, and technology. Productivity Press.

31. Reeves, M., & Deimler, M. (2011). Adaptability: The new competitive advantage. Harvard Business Review, 89(7/8), 134-141.

32. D. N. Kim, "Agile methodologies in digital transformation," International Journal of Software Engineering and Its Applications, 2018.

33. J. Womack, D. Jones, "Lean Thinking: Banish Waste and Create Wealth in Your Corporation," Free Press, 2003.

34. E. Ries, "The Lean Startup: How Today's Entrepreneurs Use Continuous Innovation to Create Radically Successful Businesses," Crown Business, 2011.

35. S. Blank, "The Four Steps to the Epiphany: Successful Strategies for Products that Win," K&S Ranch, 2013.

36. P. Senge, "The Fifth Discipline: The Art & Practice of The Learning Organization," Currency, 2006.

CHAPTER 3:

1. Westerman, G. (2018). Digital Transformation in the Age of Disruption. MIT Sloan Management Review.

2. Solis, B. (2016). The Four Pillars of Digital Transformation. Medium.

3. McAfee, A., & Brynjolfsson, E. (2017). Machine, Platform, Crowd: Harnessing Our Digital Future. W. W. Norton & Company.

4. Bass, B. M. (1985). Leadership and Performance Beyond Expectations. Free Press.

5. Burns, J. M. (1978). Leadership. Harper & Row.

6. Avolio, B. J., & Yammarino, F. J. (2002). Transformational and Charismatic Leadership: The Road Ahead. Emerald Group Publishing.

7. Adler, P. S., Goldoftas, B., & Levine, D. I. (1999). Flexibility versus efficiency? A case study of model changeovers in the Toyota production system. Organization Science, 10(1), 43-68.

8. Al-Hadid, I. A., Al-Salti, Z. N., & Al-Hadid, M. A. (2020). Factors affecting digital transformation in small and medium-sized enterprises in Jordan. Journal of Innovation and Entrepreneurship, 9(1), 1-26.

9. Bass, B. M., & Riggio, R. E. (2006). Transformational leadership. Psychology Press.

10. Bresnahan, T. F., Brynjolfsson, E., & Hitt, L. M. (2002). Information technology, workplace organization, and the demand for skilled labor: Firm-level evidence. The Quarterly Journal of Economics, 117(1), 339-376.

11. Cleveland Clinic. (2021). Cleveland Clinic Case Study. Retrieved from https://my.clevelandclinic.org/landing/

12. Eric Ries. Continuous Innovation to Create Radically Successful Businesses"

13. GE Digital. (2021). General Electric (GE) Case Study. Retrieved from https://www.ge.com/digital/case-studies/general-electric

14. George Westerman, Didier Bonnet, and Andrew McAfee "Leading Digital: Turning Technology into Business Transformation"

15. Hines, P., Holweg, M., & Rich, N. (2004). Learning to evolve: A review of contemporary lean thinking. International Journal of Operations & Production Management, 24(10), 994-1011.

16. https://ctb.ku.edu/en/table-of-contents/implement/improving-services/

17. https://hbr.org/2019/03/digital-transformation-is-not-about-technology

18. https://joinblink.com/intelligence/open-communication-importance/

19. https://leaders.com/articles/leadership/transformational-leadership/

20. https://www.ecommerce-digest.com/amazon-case-study.html

21. https://www.forbes.com/sites/benjaminlaker/2022/10/24/

22. https://www.slideshare.net/hcc79/ch-13-contemporary-issues-in-leadership

23. Kaplan, R. S., & Norton, D. P. (1996). The balanced scorecard: Translating strategy into action. Harvard Business Press.

24. Kotter, J. P. (1996). Leading change. Harvard Business Press.

25. Kouzes, J. M., & Posner, B. Z. (2017). The leadership challenge: How to make extraordinary things happen in organizations. John Wiley & Sons.

26. Lacity, M. C., & Willcocks, L. P. (2017). Nine keys to world-class business process outsourcing. Routledge.

27. Lee, C., Lee, K., & Kim, H. (2015). The impact of IT capability on innovation performance in the US healthcare industry. Health Policy and Technology, 4(2), 171-181.

28. Liker, J. K. (2004). The Toyota way: 14 management principles from the world's greatest manufacturer. McGraw-Hill.

29. Liker, J. K. (2014). The Toyota way to continuous improvement: linking strategy and operational excellence to achieve superior performance. McGraw-Hill Education.

30. Ohno, T. (1988). Toyota production system: beyond large-scale production. CRC Press.

31. Rother, M., & Shook, J. (2003). Learning to see: value-stream mapping to create value and eliminate muda. The Lean Enterprise Institute.

32. Rother, M. (2009). Toyota kata: managing people for improvement, adaptiveness, and superior results. McGraw-Hill.

33. Sabherwal, R., & Chan, Y. E. (2019). Digital transformations: Building blocks for success. Business Horizons, 62(1), 37-50.

34. Shingo, S. (1989). A study of the Toyota production system: from an industrial engineering viewpoint. CRC Press.

35. Spear, S., & Bowen, H. K. (1999). Decoding the DNA of the Toyota production system. Harvard Business Review, 77(5), 96-106.

36. Womack, J. P., Jones, D. T., & Roos, D. (1990). The machine that changed the world: The story of lean production--Toyota's secret weapon in the global car wars that is now revolutionizing world industry. Simon and Schuster.

37. Womack, J. P., Jones, D. T., & Roos, D. (1991). The machine that changed the world: the story of lean production. Free Press.

38. Womack, J. P., & Jones, D. T. (1996). Beyond Toyota: how to root out waste and pursue perfection. Harvard Business Review, 74(5), 140-157.

39. Womack, J. P., & Jones, D. T. (2003). Lean thinking: Banish waste and create wealth in your corporation. Simon and Schuster.

40. D. Kim, "Agile methodologies in digital transformation," International Journal of Software Engineering and Its Applications, 2018.

41. R. Wisner et al., "Principles of Supply Chain Management: A Balanced Approach," South-Western Cengage Learning, 2008.

42. J. Rossman, "The Amazon Way: 14 Leadership Principles Behind the World's Most Disruptive Company," Portfolio, 2014.

CHAPTER 4:

1. Womack, J. P., & Jones, D. T. (2003). Lean thinking: Banish waste and create wealth in your corporation. Simon and Schuster.

2. Ross, J. W., Beath, C. M., & Quaadgras, A. (2013). Designing the digital organization. MIT Sloan Management Review, 55(3), 27-34.

3. Rother, M., & Shook, J. (1999). Learning to see: Value stream mapping to add value and eliminate muda. Lean Enterprise Institute.

4. Westerman, G., Bonnet, D., & McAfee, A. (2014). Leading digital: Turning technology into business transformation. Harvard Business Review Press

5. Duarte, D. L., & Snyder, N. T. (2006). Mastering virtual teams: Strategies, tools, and techniques that succeed. John Wiley & Sons.

6. O'Reilly, C. A., & Tushman, M. L. (2008). Ambidexterity as a dynamic capability: Resolving the innovator's dilemma. Research in Organizational Behavior, 28, 185-206.

7. Bass, B. M., & Riggio, R. E. (2006). Transformational leadership. Psychology Press.

8. Burns, J. M. (2003). Transforming leadership: A new pursuit of happiness. Grove Press.

9. Kotter, J. P. (1996). Leading change. Harvard Business Review Press.

10. Yukl, G. A. (2013). Leadership in organizations. Pearson Education.

11. Liker, J. K. (2004). The Toyota way: 14 management principles from the world's greatest manufacturer. McGraw-Hill Education.

12. Ross, J. W., Beath, C. M., & Goodhue, D. L. (2013). Reconceptualizing firm-wide information management: From ICT adoption to digital transformation. MIS Quarterly, 38(2), 567-588.

13. Serrat, O. (2017). Understanding and developing emotional intelligence. Asian Development Bank.

14. Kotter, J. P. (2014). Accelerate: Building strategic agility for a faster-moving world. Harvard Business Review Press.

15. Liker, J. K., & Morgan, J. M. (2011). The Toyota way to continuous improvement: Linking strategy and operational excellence to achieve superior performance. McGraw-Hill Education.

16. Ross, J. W., Beath, C. M., & Quaadgras, A. (2013). The digital capability of organizations. MIT Sloan Management Review, 54(4), 61-68.

17. Westerman, G., Bonnet, D., & McAfee, A. (2014). Leading digital: Turning technology into business transformation. Harvard Business Press.

18. Siebel, T., & Gassmann, O. (2006). Seizing the white space: Business model innovation for growth and renewal. Harvard Business Press.

19. Wang, H., Chen, K., Chen, J., & Huang, S. (2017). Digital transformation of human resources in the age of big data. Human Resource Management Review, 27(2), 288-300.

20. Ranganathan, A., & Kannan, P. K. (2013). Digital marketing: A framework, review and research agenda. International Journal of Research in Marketing, 34(1), 22-45.

21. Westerman, G., Bonnet, D., & McAfee, A. (2014). Leading digital: Turning technology into business transformation. Harvard Business

22. Waller, M. A., & Fawcett, S. E. (2013). Data science, predictive analytics, and big data: A revolution that will transform supply chain design and management. Journal of Business Logistics, 34(2), 77-84.

23. Sun, H., Wang, N., & Tang, T. (2016). Understanding the impact of website quality on consumer satisfaction and purchase intention: The moderating role of website purpose. Information Systems Frontiers, 18(6), 1235-1246.

24. Hsieh, M. H., Pan, S. L., & Setiono, R. (2004). Product-service systems and information symmetry: Reducing uncertainty in online trading. Decision Support Systems, 37(3), 369-381.

25. Alagaraja, M., & Rahman, S. M. (2017). How human resource leaders can foster creativity: The mediating role of perceived organizational support. Journal of Business Research, 70, 1-9.

26. Womack, J. P., & Jones, D. T. (1996). Lean Thinking: Banish Waste and Create Wealth in Your Corporation. Free Press.

27. Ries, E. (2011). The Lean Startup: How Today's Entrepreneurs Use Continuous Innovation to Create Radically Successful Businesses. Crown Business.

28. Poppendieck, M., & Poppendieck, T. (2003). Lean Software Development: An Agile Toolkit. Addison-Wesley.

29. Blank, S. G. (2013). The Four Steps to the Epiphany: Successful Strategies for Products that Win. K&S Ranch.

30. Bass, B. M. (1985). Leadership and Performance Beyond Expectations. Free Press.

31. Ross, J. W., & Vitale, M. R. (2000). The ERP revolution: Surviving vs. thriving. InformationWeek, 80-82.

32. Bass, B. M., & Riggio, R. E. (2006). Transformational Leadership (2nd ed.). Psychology Press.

33. Ries, E. (2011). The Lean Startup: How Today's Entrepreneurs Use Continuous Innovation to Create Radically Successful Businesses. Crown Business.

34. Bass, B. M., & Avolio, B. J. (1994). Improving organizational effectiveness through transformational leadership. Thousand Oaks, CA: Sage Publications.

35. Macdonald, J., & Siwek, M. (2013). Lean Analytics: Use Data to Build a Better Startup Faster. O'Reilly Media.

36. Avolio, B. J., & Bass, B. M. (1995). Individual consideration viewed at multiple levels of analysis: A multi-level framework for examining the diffusion of transformational leadership. The Leadership Quarterly, 6(2), 199-218.

37. Davenport, T. H., Harris, J., & Shapiro, J. (2010). Competing on Talent Analytics. Harvard Business Review, 88(10), 52-58.

38. Bass, B. M., & Avolio, B. J. (1993). Transformational Leadership and Organizational Culture. Public Administration Quarterly, 17-26.

39. Avolio, B. J., & Bass, B. M. (1990). Transformational Leadership and Organizational Culture. Public Administration Quarterly, 14(1), 77-102.

40. Avolio, B. J., & Bass, B. M. (1988). Transformational Leadership, Charisma, and Beyond. In J. G. Hunt, B. R. Baliga, H. P. Dachler, & C. A. Schriesheim (Eds.), Emerging Leadership Vistas (pp. 29-49). Lexington Books.

CHAPTER 5:

1. Poppendieck, Mary. Lean Software Development: An Agile Toolkit. Addison-Wesley Professional, 2003.

2. Ries, Eric. The Lean Startup: How Today's Entrepreneurs Use Continuous Innovation to Create Radically Successful Businesses. Crown Business, 2011.

3. Lean Enterprise Institute. "Lean Digital Transformation: Case Studies." www.lean.org/digital-transformation/case-studies.

4. McKinsey & Company. "Digital Transformation: An Executive Overview." www.mckinsey.com/business-functions/mckinsey-digital/our-insights/digital-transformation-an-executive-overview.

5. Lechner, Ulrike, and Thomas Hagen. "Digitalization and Digital Transformation: Conceptual Distinctions and Contributions to Research." Proceedings of the 50th Hawaii International Conference on System Sciences, 2017.

6. Westerman, George, Didier Bonnet, and Andrew McAfee. "Leading Digital: Turning Technology into Business Transformation." Harvard Business Review Press, 2014.

7. Ross, Jeanne W., and Cynthia M. Beath. "Digitalization Requires a New Kind of Leadership." MIT Sloan Management Review, vol. 58, no. 2, 2017.

8. Loos, Peter, et al. "Digital Transformation and Industry 4.0." The International Journal of Logistics Management, vol. 29, no. 2, 2018.

9. GE Digital. "Digital Transformation: The Journey to Digital Industrial." www.ge.com/digital/journey.

10. Starbucks Corporation. "Starbucks Delivers Record Revenue & Profit Growth in Q1 FY21." www.starbucks.com/about-us/company-information/starbucks-delivers-record-revenue-and-profit-growth-in-q1-fy21.

11. Adidas AG. "Annual Report 2020." www.adidas-group.com/media/filer_public/c4/f1/c4f18479-5565-4b44-8df7-cf2b2c2d148a/adidas_gb20_en.pdf.

12. Delta Air Lines, Inc. "Annual Report 2020." www.delta.com/content/dam/delta-www/about-delta/corporate-ir/investor-relations/annual-reports/2020-annual-report.pdf.

13. Ford Motor Company. "2020 Integrated Annual Report." media.ford.com/content/dam/fordmedia/North%20America/US/2020/11/19/2020-ford-integrated-annual-report.pdf.

14. Unilever. "Sustainable Living Annual Report 2020." www.unilever.com/sustainable-living/sustainable-living-report.

15. Domino's Pizza Group plc. "2020 Annual Report." www.dominosgroup.com/media/1752/2020-domino-pizza-group-annual-report.pdf.

16. Marriott International, Inc. "2019 Annual Report." www.marriott.com/investor/documents/2019-annual-report.pdf.

17. Burberry Group plc. "Annual Report and Accounts 2020/21." www.burberryplc.com/en/newsroom/publications/annual-report.html.

18. Liker, Jeffrey K., and Gary L. Convis. "The Toyota Way to Lean Leadership: Achieving and Sustaining Excellence Through Leadership Development." McGraw-Hill Education, 2011.

19. Brandt, Steven D., and Charles A. Conrad. "The Lean IT Field Guide: A Roadmap for Your Transformation." Productivity Press, 2015.

20. Fernie, John, and David B. Grant. "Logistics and Retail Management: Emerging Issues and New Challenges in the Retail Supply Chain." Kogan Page Publishers, 2015.

21. Holler, Jens X., et al. "Implementing Lean Six Sigma in the Siemens Industry Sector." The TQM Journal, vol. 24, no. 1, 2012.

22. Davenport, Thomas H. "Process Innovation: Reengineering Work Through Information Technology." Harvard Business Press, 1993.

23. GE Aviation. "Digital Solutions." www.geaviation.com/digital-solutions.

24. Baudin, Michel. "Lean Assembly: The Nuts and Bolts of Making Assembly Operations Flow." CRC Press, 2010.

25. Hines, Peter, and Nick Rich. "The Seven Value Stream Mapping Tools." Routledge, 2018.

26. Walton, Sam, and John Huey. "Made in America: My Story." Bantam Books, 1993.

27. Singh, Prabhjot, and Thomas H. Davenport. "Healthcare Delivery Reform and Big Data: Balancing Digital and Human Ingenuity." Business Horizons, vol. 59, no. 6, 2016.

28. Kwon, Ilro, et al. "An Integrated Vehicle Routing and Inventory Management System for Perishable Products." International Journal of Production Economics, vol. 139, no. 1, 2012.

29. Reinhart, Gunther, et al. "Maintenance and Repair in the Fourth Industrial Revolution: A Digital Approach." Procedia Manufacturing, vol. 11, 2017.

30. Mason-Jones, Rachel, and David R. Towill. "Lean, Agile, Resilient, and Green: The Path to Supply Chain Excellence." CRC Press, 2007.

31. Akter, S., Wamba, S. F., Gunasekaran, A., Dubey, R., & Childe, S. J. (2016). How to improve firm performance using big data analytics capability and business strategy alignment? International Journal of Production Economics, 182, 113-131.

32. Amazon.(n.d.).About Amazon - Our Company. Retrieved from https://www.amazon.com/p/feature/rzekmvyjojcp6uc

33. Blank, S. (2013). Why the Lean Start-Up Changes Everything. Harvard Business Review, 91(5), 63-72.

34. Bolívar-Ramos, M. T., &García-Morales, V. J. (2016).Relationship between entrepreneurial orientation and the creation of a culture of innovation: The role of organizational learning. Journal of Business Research, 69(5), 2027-2031.

35. Bosch. (n.d.).Connected manufacturing. Retrieved from
    https://www.bosch.com/stories/connected-manufacturing/

36. Cognizant. (2017). Digitalization vs. Digitization: Why the Difference Matters.
    Retrieved   from   https://www.cognizant.com/whitepapers/digitalization-vs-
    digitization-why-the-difference-matters-codex2305.pdf

37. Digital Transformation - Statistics & Facts, Statista,
    https://www.statista.com/topics/2442/digital-transformation/

38. "Digital transformation: What it is, why it matters, and what the big trends
    are", McKinsey & Company, https://www.mckinsey.com/business-
    functions/mckinsey-digital/our-insights/digital-transformation-what-it-is-why-
    it-matters-and-what-the-big-trends-are

39. "Digitalization, Digitization, and Digital Transformation: Confuse Them at
    Your Peril", Forbes,
    https://www.forbes.com/sites/jasonbloomberg/2017/10/12/digitalization-
    digitization-and-digital-transformation-confuse-them-at-your-
    peril/?sh=4fa3e3a67de9

40. "Digitization vs. Digitalization: What's the Difference?", Adobe,
    https://www.adobe.com/express/learn/creative-cloud/digitization-vs-
    digitalization/

41. "Digital Transformation Examples: The 7 Pillars Of Success", Forbes,
    https://www.forbes.com/sites/danielnewman/2017/01/24/digital-
    transformation-examples-the-7-pillars-of-success/?sh=2cd2d9c47177

42. Gao, R., & Sharma, R. (2018). Digital transformation of business models—Best
    practice, enablers, and roadmap. Journal of Business Research, 89, 334-346.

43. Gulliver, S. (2019). What is Lean Digital? And how can it improve your
    business?. Retrieved from https://www.raconteur.net/business-innovation/lean-
    digital

44. Haier.(n.d.).Innovation ecosystem. Retrieved from
    https://www.haier.net/en/about_haier/innovation_ecosystem/

45. Houtman, K. (2020). The Netflix approach to digital transformation:
    Continuous innovation. Retrieved from
    https://www.forbes.com/sites/kimberlyhoutman/2020/07/08/the-netflix-
    approach-to-digital-transformation-continuous-innovation/?sh=3c85cd0b3c68

46. Lean Enterprise Institute. (n.d.).Value-Stream Mapping. Retrieved from
    https://www.lean.org/LeanPost/Posting.cfm?LeanPostId=512

47. Lean Digital: The Key to a Successful Digital Transformation, BCG
    (https://www.bcg.com/en-au/publications/2020/lean-digital-the-key-to-a-
    successful-digital-transformation)

48. Li, Y., & Li, H. (2018).A conceptual model of enterprise digital transformation. Journal of Business Research, 88, 282-288.

49. Liker, J. K. (2004). The Toyota Way: 14 management principles from the world's greatest manufacturer. McGraw-Hill.

50. McMillon, D. (2020). Our Strategy. Retrieved from https://corporate.walmart.com/our-story/our-strategy

51. Microsoft.(n.d.).Walmart transforms retail with Microsoft AI to empower associates and improve customer service. Retrieved from https://customers.microsoft.com/en-us/story/780747-walmart-retail-azure-iot-ai

52. Poppendieck, M., &Poppendieck, T. (2003). Lean software development: an agile toolkit. Addison-Wesley Professional.

53. Ries, E. (2011). The Lean Startup: How Today's Entrepreneurs Use Continuous Innovation to Create Radically Successful Businesses. Crown Business.

54. "Scaling Agile @ Spotify with Tribes, Squads, Chapters & Guilds," by HenrikKniberg and Anders Ivarsson, Agile Product Ownership in a Nutshell, October 2012.

55. Siemens.(n.d.).Digital twin. Retrieved from https://new.siemens.com/global/en/products/automation/industry-software/digital-enterprise-suites/digital-twin.html

56. Singh, A., Singh, A., &Rai, A. (2019).Digital transformation: A review and synthesis. Journal of Business Research, 99, 365-377.

57. Trefis Team. (2020). How Walmart is investing in its supply chain. Retrieved from https://www.forbes.com/sites/greatspeculations/2020/08/24/how-walmart-is-investing-in-its-supply-chain/?sh=19d2282e2d8b

58. Tung, L. (2018). Digitization, digitalization, and digital transformation: Confuse them at your peril. ZDNet. Retrieved from https://www.zdnet.com/article/digitization-digitalization-and-digital-transformation-confuse-them-at-your-peril/

59. What is Lean Digital? And Why You Need it in Your Business, JTC (https://www.jtc.org/blog/what-is-lean-digital-and-why-you-need-it-in-your-business/)

60. Womack, J. P., & Jones, D. T. (2003). Lean thinking: Banish waste and create wealth in your corporation. Simon and Schuster.

CHAPTER 6:

1. Kary, M. (2017). The Four Principles of Lean Management. Leanpub.

2. Radziwill, N. M. (2018). Lean Digital: The rise of lean thinking in the digital era. Quality Management Journal, 25(2), 6-22.

3. Reinertsen, D. G. (2009). The Principles of Product Development Flow: Second Generation Lean Product Development. Celeritas Publishing.

4. Sutherland, J., & Schwaber, K. (2017). The Scrum Guide. Scrum.org

5. Ross, J. W., Beath, C. M., & Quaadgras, A. (2019). Designed for digital: How to architect your business for sustained success.

6. Hines, P., & Found, P. (2019). Lean Digital transformation: How to drive agility and customer centricity.

7. Evans, J. R., & Dalkir, K. (2019). The digital transformation playbook: Rethink your business for the digital age.

8. Womack, J. P., & Jones, D. T. (2018). Lean thinking: Banish waste and create wealth in your corporation.

9. Immelt, J. R., Govindarajan, V., & Trimble, C. (2016). How GE is disrupting itself. Harvard Business Review.

10. Doyle, J. (2020). Domino's Pizza: A case study in organizational evolution. Forbes.

11. Salesforce. (n.d.). Trailblazer Community.

12. Netflix. (n.d.). Company Overview.

13. British Broadcasting Corporation. (2014). BBC Digital Strategy.

14. Adobe. (n.d.). Adobe Digital Academy.

15. Google. (n.d.). Company - Our Culture.

16. Spotify Engineering Culture. (n.d.).

17. Tesla. (n.d.). About Tesla.

18. Amazon. (n.d.). Personalize the customer experience.

19. Brown, T. (2008). Design Thinking. Harvard Business Review.

20. Norman, D. A. (2013). The Design of Everyday Things. "Iterative Progress: Embracing Continuous Improvement in the Digital Era"

21. Poppendieck, M., & Poppendieck, T. (2003). Lean Software Development: An Agile Toolkit.

22. O'Reilly, T. (2013). What's the Future of Business?: Changing the Way Businesses Create Experiences.

23. Liker, J. K. (2004). The Toyota Way: 14 Management Principles from the World's Greatest Manufacturer.

24. Ries, E. (2011). The Lean Startup: How Today's Entrepreneurs Use Continuous Innovation to Create Radically Successful Businesses.

25. Reeves, M., Levin, S., & Ueda, D. (2016). The Biology of Corporate Survival.

26. Nonaka, I., & Takeuchi, H. (1995). The Knowledge-Creating Company: How Japanese Companies Create the Dynamics of Innovation.

27. Mayer-Schönberger, V., & Cukier, K. (2013). Big Data: A Revolution That Will Transform How We Live, Work, and Think.

28. Brynjolfsson, E., & McAfee, A. (2014). The Second Machine Age: Work, Progress, and Prosperity in a Time of Brilliant Technologies.

29. Poppendieck, M., & Poppendieck, T. (2003). Lean software development: An agile toolkit. Pearson Education.

30. Liker, J. K. (2004). The Toyota way: 14 management principles from the world's greatest manufacturer. McGraw-Hill Education.

31. Ohno, T. (1988). Toyota production system: beyond large-scale production. CRC Press.

32. Liker, J. K., & Franz, J. K. (2011). The Toyota way to continuous improvement: linking strategy and operational excellence to achieve superior performance. McGraw-Hill Education.

33. Singh, R. K., & Garg, S. K. (2020). Lean Digital transformation: a guide to transform business processes. Springer.

34. Duhigg, C. (2016). Smarter Faster Better: The Secrets of Being Productive in Life and Business. Random House.

Appendix

1. Radnor, Z., & Johnston, R. (2018). Lean in public services: Panacea or paradox? Public Administration, 96(4), 808-822.

2. Ross, J. W., Beath, C. M., & Quaadgras, A. (2013). Strategic principles for competing in the digital age. MIT Sloan Management Review, 55(2), 37-44.

3. Shingo, S.

In what ways can the status quo be challenged?

1. Womack, J. P., & Jones, D. T. (2003). Lean thinking: Banish waste and create wealth in your corporation. Simon and Schuster.

2. Bhasin, S. (2019). The Lean Digital Transformation Playbook: Rethink How to Gain Market Share by Streamlining Processes with Digital Innovation. Apress.

3. Ries, E. (2011). The Lean Startup: How Today's Entrepreneurs Use Continuous Innovation to Create Radically Successful Businesses. Crown Business.

Author's Note

Navigating Lean Digital Transformation: People First, Tech Second

The information provided in this book is intended to offer insights into Lean Digital Transformation with a focus on prioritizing people over technology. While every effort has been made to ensure the accuracy and completeness of the content, we acknowledge the possibility of unintentional errors, omissions, or oversights.

Readers are encouraged to use their discretion and consult additional sources when making decisions based on the content presented. The references cited in the book are provided for further exploration and verification.

If you have any questions, concerns, or feedback regarding the content, or if you believe there may be missing references or other issues, we welcome your input. Please feel free to contact us via email at gouravdudeja@gmail.com. Your feedback is valuable, and we are committed to addressing any discrepancies or oversights promptly and positively.

This book is intended to serve as a resource for leadership, aiming to contribute to the discourse on Lean Digital Transformation. It is not a substitute for professional advice, and the authors disclaim any liability arising directly or indirectly from the use of the information provided.

Thank you for your understanding and for being a part of this journey towards effective and people-centric leadership.

Sincerely,

Gourav Dudeja

Author Introduction

Gourav Dudeja is an accomplished author and seasoned professional with over 20 years of diverse experience in the corporate world. As the Vice President of Commercial Operations & Strategy for a fast growing FMCG company, he spearheads transformative strategies and initiatives that drive commercial success and operational excellence.

Gourav's impressive journey has spanned renowned organizations such as Denso, Robert Bosch, ABB, Bombardier & Avantor, where he has consistently delivered exceptional results globally. His academic background is equally notable, boasting a PGDBA in Operations Management, an MBA in Finance and Supply Chain Management, and ongoing doctoral research at Amity University. His commitment to excellence is further underscored by his certification as a Master Black Belt and a plethora of other certifications and training achievements.

Throughout his illustrious career, Gourav has collaborated closely with C-suite executives from diverse functional areas, leveraging his expertise in Lean, Six Sigma, Digital Transformation, and other related tools to create substantial impact. His guiding philosophy, "People before process," encapsulates his belief in the paramount importance of human capital in navigating the complexities of the modern VUCA (Volatile, Uncertain, Complex, and Ambiguous) world.

In his book, "Navigating Lean Digital Transformation: People First, Tech Second," Gourav shares his wealth of knowledge and insights, offering a roadmap for success in the ever-evolving digital landscape. His passion for enhancing people and leadership shines through, promising to create significant value for organizations and individuals alike.